Bessie Head, one of Africa's be
born in South Africa in 1937
1986, leaving behind her a fine coll
Tenderness and Power was the first of
her death, and another anthology,
published posthumously. Both thes
literary achievements, already evident in her novels *When Rain Clouds Gather*, *Maru* and *A Question of Power*, the short story collection *The Collector of Treasures* and her historical account *Serowe: Village of the Rain Wind*, which are all available in the Heinemann African Writers Series.

BESSIE HEAD

TALES OF TENDERNESS AND POWER

HEINEMANN

Heinemann International
a division of Heinemann Educational Books Ltd
Halley Court, Jordan Hill, Oxford OX2 8EJ

Heinemann Educational Books Inc
361 Hanover Street, Portsmouth, New Hampshire, 03801, USA

Heinemann Educational Books (Nigeria) Ltd
PMB 5205, Ibadan
Heinemann Kenya Ltd
Kijabe Street, PO Box 45314, Nairobi
Heinemann Educational Boleswa
PO Box 10103, Village Post Office, Gaborone, Botswana
Heinemann Publishers (Caribbean) Ltd
175 Mountain View Avenue, Kingston 6, Jamaica

LONDON EDINBURGH MELBOURNE SYDNEY
AUCKLAND SINGAPORE HARARE
MADRID ATHENS BOLOGNA

British Library Cataloguing in Publication Data

Head, Bessie, 1937–1986
Tales of tenderness and power.
I. Title   II. Series
823 [F]

ISBN 0–435–90579–1

Printed in Great Britain by
Cox and Wyman Ltd, Reading

90 91 92 93 94 10 9 8 7 6 5 4 3 2 1

CONTENTS

INTRODUCTION **7**

Let me tell a story now . . .   **16**

Oranges and Lemons   **19**

Snowball   **28**

Sorrow food   **32**

Chibuku Beer and Independence   **37**

Village People   **41**

The old woman   **42**

Summer sun   **44**

The green tree   **45**

Tao   **48**

The Woman from America   **56**

Chief Sekoto holds Court   **61**

Property   **65**

A Power Struggle   **72**

A Period of Darkness   **78**

The Lovers   **84**

The General   **102**

Son of the Soil   **116**

The Prisoner who Wore Glasses   **125**

The Coming of the Christ-Child   **131**

Dreamer and Storyteller   **141**

ACKNOWLEDGEMENTS   **144**

INTRODUCTION

Bessie Head was born in South Africa in 1937, but she lived almost half her life in Serowe, Botswana, where she died in 1986. She sometimes complained to her friends that she was often forced to reel off the facts of her early life: 'I was born in Pietermaritzburg in 1937 . . . my mother died in a mental institution . . . I was educated at a mission school outside Durban . . .' — so mechanically that these events became more and more unreal to her.

If she tried to avoid thinking of her childhood, and she certainly spent most of her life doing just this, it is very understandable. Her background could hardly have been more traumatic. The daughter of a wealthy white woman and the family's black stable hand, she was born after her mother had been admitted to a mental hospital. She was given out to a white family by the unsuspecting adoption authorities, but was soon returned because she looked 'strange'. After that she was adopted by a so-called 'coloured' couple. Her adopted father died when she was about six, around the same time her own mother died, and seven years later, with conditions in the home deteriorating, she was sent to St Monica's Home, Hillary, by the Child Welfare authorities.

She still believed herself to be the child of the family she had grown up with, but when the first holidays approached and she thought she would be going 'home' to her 'mother', she suffered a severe shock. Showing an appalling lack of insight, the principal told her that she would never be going to that house again. Her so-called mother was not her real mother. Her real mother was a white woman. She was insane. Bessie had better be careful or she might end up insane too. Her mother had had to be locked up because she was having an affair with a stable boy, who was a native.

This is the gist of what was revealed to her, as she herself records it later in interviews. In the course of a few minutes this series of mind-shattering facts was forced upon her. She was, as I have mentioned, thirteen at the time. In later life she attributed her dislike of missionaries and her distrust of

Christianity to this and other encounters she had with the principal who was there when she arrived at the school. Nonetheless, she did meet one person at St Monica's who inspired her so much that she named the main character in her second novel after her.

This character's name is Margaret Cadmore. Though a San (or 'Bushman' as she would have been called), she is brought up and given an excellent education by a missionary of the same name. Shortly after this second novel *Maru* was published, Bessie Head received a letter from an English doctor, expressing interest in the name. She told Bessie that she had had a friend named Margaret Cadmore, who had worked as a missionary in South Africa after doing active service as a nurse during the Second World War. Bessie Head wrote back:

> Your school friend was the Margaret Cadmore of my book. She became principal of St Monica's Home in Hillary when I was a pupil there. I did not have such a close relationship with her such as I outlined in my book but I did love her for her personality. Any very vivid, wayward, free person is very attractive to me and makes a deep impression I never forget (BHP, file 149, 24.5.72).

Bessie Head's mother had left written instructions that her daughter was to be given a good education, and the mission school lived up to these instructions to the best of its ability. She acquired, with her knowledge of daffodils, snowdrops and other English flowers then seldom seen on the African continent, a thorough knowledge of the English lake poets and Dickens and a great love for books and reading generally. 'The rest I did myself later', she said in 1984, summing up this period of her life. After gaining a Natal Teachers' Senior Certificate in 1955, she taught for a few years in Durban before moving to Cape Town and later to Johannesburg, where she worked as a journalist. When she turned 21, she was paid out a small lump sum, the remains of the amount her mother had left her for her education.

During her short life Bessie Head published six full-length works and about 25 short stories. Nearly everything she wrote relates to her years in Botswana. She was a writer who won early international acclaim. Her first novel, *When Rain Clouds Gather* (1969), was received with enthusiasm by critics in America and England. The same applied to *Maru*, which was regarded by many as even better than her first. However, the reactions to her third novel, *A Question of Power*, were very mixed. Puzzled critics and readers alike tried to understand the predicament of the tortured protagonist, Elizabeth, caught up in a direct confrontation with Good and Evil, God and the Devil, in Head's powerful portrayal of a woman in the throes of a nervous breakdown. Today most critics agree that *A Question of Power* is her greatest work. It was on the short list for the Booker Prize in 1974, its year of publication, and sold surprisingly well. Nevertheless, for Bessie then it heralded a time of uncertainty and increasing financial instability. Having written three novels of a clearly autobiographical nature, she was suddenly given the chance to turn her attention towards the community in which she lived.

She began on her Serowe project, the writing of a semi-documentary account of the village and its history. She decided to shape the book around interviews with people of all age groups and occupations and when she was finished she had created a living memento to the largest village in Africa south of the Sahara. *Serowe: Village of the Rain Wind* was published, finally, in 1981. Prior to that, Head's first collection of short stories appeared: *The Collector of Treasures and other Botswana Village Tales* (1977). She often said that these tales were the spilling over of the interviews with the village people she had done for the Serowe book. They focus chiefly on ordinary (or extraordinary) village women and their problems. In 1984 Bessie Head published the last book she was to write. It is entitled *A Bewitched Crossroad* and has clear links to the preceding ones. Here she traces the history of Africa seen from a black, not a white point of view. She focuses especially on the Bamangwato tribe and its famous chieftain, Khama III, who lived in Serowe and lies buried there with his successors, including his grandson, Seretse Khama.

The present anthology represents the second collection of Bessie Head's shorter writings. They cannot all be classified as short stories in the usual use of that designation: some are short descriptive observations, some are fictional or semi-fictional, some historical stories. But most of them have one thing in common. They are closely-rooted in actual events. The only purely fictional story is 'The General'. Even in 'Chief Sekoto Holds Court', the incident described is probably based on fact, though Head has shaped the events to her own purpose. All the others are stories clearly related to or identifiable with personal, national or historical events, or we have her word for it that the story is based on fact.

The short introductory piece from 1962 with which the anthology begins is thus very characteristic of Bessie Head's style. She enjoyed observing, smiling, forgiving or raging and then recording. She could be regarded as a genuine teller of tales, part of an ancient African tradition, and she liked to refer to her short stories as tales. As can be seen from the full title of her first short story collection, she regarded these as 'Botswana Village Tales'. Later, she worked on a group of stories she called her 'historical tales', represented in this anthology with 'A Power Struggle', 'A Period of Darkness', 'The Lovers', and 'Son of the Soil'.

Often choosing a mundane event as her starting point, then, Bessie Head proceeds to give her story a subtle lift, even universal significance as she, the teller of tales, intrudes with humorous comments or her own view of things. Often she introduces an element of tenderness to the original event. She was easily moved by a generous action and responded quickly to real goodness, which she continued to believe does exist, especially in the lives of ordinary people. Yet she had, as well, a sharp nose for the power people, whom she exposed at every opportunity.

Some of the historical tales illustrate these traits. Of 'A Power Struggle' she writes in 1977:

The story deals with a period before the colonial era. Fierce jealousies and greed surrounded the position of king and chieftainship but I worked behind that over to a strange philosophical beauty people displayed . . . A good man always has a weak position and lacks the kind of power that an evil man has. He gets killed and forced out of the tribe. Then the people would take over and as if the man was still alive, a whole section of the people would go after him. They would abandon evil (BHP, file 15, 23.6.77).

Writing about 'A Period of Darkness' earlier the same year, she says: 'It's a polemic on the fact that a ruler is only in existence because he has people to rule; thus the people are of greater importance than the ruler (BHP, file 15, 23.1.77)'. She then refers at great length to an incident she had come across while doing research for her Khama III novel: the assassination by his own tribe of the southern Botswana chief Motswalele II because he did not observe this rule.

Another historical tale, 'The Lovers', is Head's version of Botswana's only great love legend about two young people, some three hundred years ago, who allowed themselves to be carried away by their passions and thus threw their community into chaos. After they were expelled from the village, they disappeared altogether and a terrible fear grew up that a hill nearby had opened and swallowed them. To this day 'the hill has been invested with supernatural powers and no black person will set foot on it . . . The love story so haunted me that I could find no peace until I had written my story of it. Sanely, a hill could never open and swallow people so my story dwells on what happened before the lovers disappeared so mysteriously', wrote Bessie Head of this tale in 1977.

Bessie Head liked a sense of continuity. When she was working on the stories in *The Collector of Treasures* she wrote to her publisher that the order in which the stories appeared was very important. Because she saw the collection as a unit, she was able to shape the individual stories in such a way that one trailed into the other. Such close links cannot be established in the present collection. However, some attention has been given to the way the stories have been grouped. Chronology is considered, of course. Thus the first four short pieces are some of the earliest she wrote and originate from her days in Cape Town. Later she criticises her own moralising tone in 'Oranges and Lemons' — 'rather high-handed and shrill' she calls it — but she also verifies the truth of incident 'worked down to a simple sordid level — when people are trapped they do unbelievable things (BHP, file 75, 4.1.74)'.

When Bessie Head left South Africa in 1964 taking her young son with her after a broken marriage, she left on an exit pass, never to return. Though she took up a teaching post in Serowe on arrival, she gave it up again after a year and from 1965 to 1968 she lived in Francistown, part of the refugee community. Later she moved back to Serowe and of this period of her life she writes:

> The accommodation I had in Francistown was a palace compared to what I have here. Serowe is an enormous village of 33,000 people (now 45,000 Ed.) who all live in mud huts. I too at the moment and it is a small circular room in which I have to cook, wash and eat. There is no space to spread out my files, notes and working materials without their becoming covered with layers and layers of dust. Many insects also make their abode in the grass thatching and calmly submit their droppings all over the place (BHP, file 60, 18.6.69).

The next seven short pieces in the anthology were written during this early period of her life in Serowe. She was desperately poor, living on help from international refugee organisations, yet she retained her sense of humour and her eye for the strange complexities of life. No doubt she had totally abandoned her literary ambitions but she did submit 'The Woman from America' to *The New Statesman* where it was published in 1966. Two years later, early in 1968, the same story appeared in *Classic*, an American magazine. An editor from an American publishing house happened to read it and wrote to Bessie Head asking her for some longer stories. When Bessie wrote back saying that she could not afford to buy writing materials, the Simon & Schuster editor sent her $80 and told her to start writing. She was just becoming interested in one of the first experiments in rural development in Serowe, started by the regent chief of the Bangwato,

Tshekedi Khama, with help from an English agriculturalist and this provided the idea behind *When Rain Clouds Gather*. A reshaped excerpt from this novel is included in this anthology as 'Chief Sekoto Holds Court'.

After this extract, come the historical tales. Except for 'Property', which is somewhat older and unpublished, they were written in the middle of the seventies. They provided Bessie with a fresh interest when she felt herself weighed down with the problems connected with the publishing of *Serowe: Village of the Rain Wind* and her difficult research for the Khama novel. What is more, she very much hoped that they would sell easily as she was very poor. She worked hard on them all, complaining about not being able to get beyond the opening lines of one because she had high ambitions for the story, or admitting that she had cried for several days because another would not work out. She also had high hopes for 'The Lovers'. She thought it a beautiful story and expected it to be published without delay. 'I usually know when I have a good thing going', she wrote to a friend. But it circulated for a long time without being accepted.

The last five stories relate more directly to the present. Bessie Head's own lack of a family, her many years of historical research, her life in a rural area of a free African state clearly play their part in focusing her attention on the soil as a symbol of a person's roots and identity. In a rural community, soil and identity are one. Hence her powerful account of the loss of this identity for black South Africans in 'Son of the Soil'. This story reflects her great admiration for Sol T. Plaatje, one of those 'elegant British educated black men' who had formed part of the Native National Congress delegation in 1914 to protest over the Natives' Land Act. The only other story in the anthology that seems never to have been previously published is 'The General', refreshing in its understated humour and penetrating insight. 'The Prisoner Who Wore Glasses' is probably one of Bessie Head's best known short stories apart from those in *The Collector of Treasures*. It has appeared in at least three anthologies since its original publication in *London Magazine* in 1973, and has also been translated into Danish, Dutch and German. Again

13

Bessie vouches for its authenticity. A young political refugee whom she got to know during her time in Francistown told her how they had humanised a gaoler while he was a political prisoner in South Africa. She admits that she has embroidered the tale, adding what she calls 'certain tendernesses', but the story is a true one.

The penultimate story in the collection is in reality a tribute. Bessie Head wrote it shortly after the death of Robert Sobukwe, of whom she later said: '(His) view of Pan Africanism gave me a comfortable black skin to live in and work with'. She admitted once that she did not so much admire the movement as a whole as him personally, and after his death she did ponder on the effect that a position of power could have had on his personality. In 'The Coming of the Christ Child', however, she pays homage to Sobukwe's integrity and powers of leadership; here he represents her ideal political leader, as Khama III also does. The taut style of the story, the simmering indignation, the careful preparation for the significance of the title, mark this as a story produced under emotional pressure. She knew of the Xhosa tradition of sitting quietly at midnight each Christmas Eve to await the coming of the Christ Child and she chose the title because she knew that Robert was a Xhosa by birth.

Bessie Head said of herself in 1983 that 'political and religious matters are not lacking in my work except that I have not dealt with them in the usual way (BHP, file 184, 9.11.1983)'. 'The Coming of the Christ Child' and many other stories in this anthology are good illustrations of that remark.

Bessie Head always retained her individualism. Though feeling strongly about racism and sexual discrimination – and having gained by the bitterest experience a considerable knowledge of both problems – she would never allow herself to be totally identified with either African nationalism or feminism. Her vision included whites and blacks, men and women. What she feared was the misuse of power, what she strove towards was human goodness and love. The idea of the basic goodness and decency of the ordinary person never left her. Though she became increasingly susceptible to the evil around her as she grew older, including the constant misuse of power at local, national and international levels, she clung bravely to her ideals. This often made her feel isolated. Her quiet village life became a retreat for her then.

When she died in April 1986 she was engaged in writing her autobiography. Unfortunately she had not reached the stage where some form of posthumous publication would have been possible. But she left something else: an enormous collection of letters. Bessie Head made carbon copies of nearly all the letters she wrote and kept nearly all the letters she received in classified order. She corresponded avidly with her publishers, agents, literary contacts and friends from all over the world. She was a lively and deeply-engaged letter writer and there is no doubt that her correspondence, when it appears in print, will enhance her stature as a writer. Time may indeed show that the universal truths of her message presented in her own highly individualistic way will give her a very prominent place among writers on the African continent. So it is hoped that this anthology, presenting as it does so much material that has never been published in book form before, and representing the first of Bessie Head's writings to appear since her death, will honour her memory, reinforce her literary status and, in its own right, provide pleasure for the reader.

Gillian Stead Eilersen, 1989

Note: The Bessie Head Papers (BHP) have been bought and catalogued by the Khama III Memorial Museum, Serowe, Botswana. The extracts of letters quoted in this introduction have been taken from that collection. See 'The Bessie Head Papers: Some Preliminary Comments' by Gillian Stead Eilersen, *Botswana Notes and Records*, 1988, Box 71, Gaborone.

Let me tell a story now . . .

I don't know why this is so but the first thing a person you've just been introduced to will ask you is: 'What work do you do?' I don't mean that he or she will ask it bluntly, just like that. They will hedge around a bit but eventually they will get down to the point and drag it out of you. As I say, I don't know why you dare to ask such a personal question but the reason that I do is because each person that I meet is a complete mystery to me. I have to find a quick and super-ficial way of piecing him together so that I know where I stand. I mean, I don't like to behave like a fool and some people instantly give you the feeling that you are behaving like a fool. I'm specifically referring to a hard case lawyer I once knew. I struggled quite unsuccessfully to explain a delicate matter to him that needed just a bit of understand-ing and humane feeling and couldn't understand why he kept pulling me to shreds. Only later I learnt that the man's mind worked this way: 'Let's consider it on a judicial basis.' The poor man had completely identified himself with his work. He was all one-sided. A very dangerous type that because they can bust your ego to bits and you won't know what's happening to you, especially if your enemies are around and watching the terrible beating you are taking from one who knows all the answers.

In a broad sense then I would say a person's character type makes him gravitate to a certain type of work. The fussy-fussy, jumpy sort of woman becomes a typist where she can mess around all day minding other people's businesses. The rather heartless, dominating you-actually-deserve-all-you-get type becomes a social worker. The tough guy with sadistic tendencies becomes a jail warder or a policeman. The dull, drab and toiling type a waitress, shop-girl or nurse. And so on.

I'm sorry but it has taken me quite a long time to get down to what I actually wanted to say. When anyone asked me this question, namely: 'What work do you do?' I used to answer: 'Oh, I'm a writer'. Which is quite a lie because I've hardly written a thing, and I've tried but I know I just wouldn't be able to earn a living by writing. Working people are earning a living. I won't truthfully be a writer until I'm *earning* something from the business.

When they said: 'Oh, that's interesting and what have you written?' I would say: 'Well . . . I have two unpublished manuscripts. One got lost in the post. The other got lost among the papers and rubble on a publisher's desk.' Nobody believed me, of course, and funnily enough I was telling the truth. I didn't have the guts to defend myself because I wouldn't have liked them to read what I had written. It was a hotch-potch of under-done ideas, and, monotonous in the extreme. There was always a Coloured man here, an African man there and a White somewhere around the corner. Always the same old pattern. I tried to be poetic but even that didn't help. I just bored myself to death and I assumed that I would bore others too so I shut my mouth pretty quick about what I had written. If I had to write one day I would just like to say *people is people* and not damn White, damn Black. Perhaps if I was a good enough writer I could still write damn White, damn Black and still make people *live*. Make them real. Make you love them, not because of the colour of their skin but because they are important as human beings.

For instance, I would like to write the story about a man who is a packing hand at the railways and lives in one of the tumbling down, leaky houses in District Six. One year for his annual leave he decided to make use of the railway concession and take a free train ride with his wife to Durban. All the neighbours knew about it because they are a popular and sociable couple, as are most people in District Six. No one has much of a private life in District Six. The neighbours make it their business to know all about you and they don't mind what your sins are. In fact, if it comes to the push they'll defend you even if the law considers you in the wrong. The only suspicious man in District Six is the man who doesn't show his face and keeps a closed door. We are

17

the real good and jolly neighbours, minding each other's business the way neighbours should. We can't help it because we're all piled up on each other.

Well, to get back to the story. This man and his wife had a crowd of friends tagging along as they went to catch the train to Durban. Ticket and booking all arranged. Bags stacked with food for the journey. Things like roast fowl, fish cakes, meat balls and plenty of sandwiches and some booze. The wife, a huge, adventurous, generous, loud-talking, happy and carefree woman climbed on the train first. The husband remained on the platform with the friends. He was sort of glum with a I'm-figuring-this-thing-out look on his face. He always gets that look on his face when he's not too pleased about something. Just as the first warning bell rang he shouted with real terror in his voice: 'Ma, get off. Let's go home.' And that was that. He didn't even have to explain. Everyone understood. To leave Cape Town and go gallivanting around like some fool in a foreign place like Durban would be an act of the most vile treachery. Cape Town is his home. He was born here. He will die here. Besides, nobody in Durban would understand him. He has a very special kind of language. His very own. He has a special kind of face that is comfortingly reflected in the faces around him. Those faces swear with the exact same nuance that he does. They eat the exact same food. They have the exact same humour. Why go to that fool of a place called Durban? What is there in it for him? To leave Cape Town would be like dying. It would be the destruction of all that he is as a man. He just doesn't have the kind of pretentiousness that makes an American tourist come and gape at the Zulu dances.

Well there it is. I would like to write the story of the man and his wife who never took the train journey, but I can't. When I think of writing any single thing I panic and go dead inside. Perhaps it's because I have my ear too keenly attuned to the political lumberjacks who are busy making capital on human lives. Perhaps I'm just having nightmares. Whatever my manifold disorders are, I hope to get them sorted out pretty soon, because *I've just got to tell a story*.

Oranges and Lemons

The township was some twenty miles outside Johannesburg. It was built in the shape of a vast out-spreading horse shoe. The only pretty thing about the whole area was the soft blue dome of sky that stretched from one wide sweeping horizon to another. Otherwise, not a flower bloomed in the cramped tiny spaces between the innumerable and identical small match-box houses.

Whenever there was a bank hold-up in the city, the newspapers set up a hue and cry about conditions in the township. They were in the habit of referring to it as a place of 'crime and bloodshed'. They printed gruesome pictures of permanently maimed residents together with the sharp thin-bladed knives that had pierced their spinal cords. The police, who conducted almost daily raids on the township said much the same thing. But it was only the people who lived in it who were fully aware of its fearful evil and viciousness. And they were helplessly trapped in one long dark nightmare without end. Few resisted the evil and these few were swiftly eliminated, perhaps through their innocence of evil.

Things had come to such a pass, no mother could ever be sure that her young daughter would reach the age of eighteen without being either raped a thousand times, or murdered and murder was almost daily fare. And perhaps the mothers even got used to it. Funerals had a prestige value; all the crying and fainting and sensationalism were talking points for weeks and weeks until some more sensational happening pushed yours into the background. Few happenings really shocked or troubled the residents of the township. One of them was the murder of Old Ben. The other was the story of the ruin of Jimmy Motsisi and it was the way in which they recounted these two stories and sighed heavily that caused a faint ray of hope in this bottomless pit of darkness; that perhaps people would arise one day and through sheer force of will, shut this evil up in the terrible dark caverns of the earth forever.

Some people say it is all caused by the political ills of the country and that once these wrongs have been righted, the evil will vanish overnight. Others doubt this. They say that a man's actions create his destiny which destiny he must reap in due course.

Old Ben lingered on in the mind as his name had become synonymous with the Sunday roast in a large number of households in the township. He worked for a butchery in the city and on Saturday afternoons he would make the rounds, delivering special orders for the Sunday dinner. Things were not always so good. Maybe the breadwinner in the family had had his wages stolen. Maybe he had deserted. Maybe he was killed. But the meat was delivered all the same even if this kindness made Old Ben's pocket empty. And it was a little more than that; the way he could come into a poky little house as though the sun was entering the doorway. And he had a queer, memorable laugh. He'd raise one big right hand in the air and throw back his head and neigh like a horse.

Early one Sunday morning Old Ben was found sprawled on his back in the road, dead, in a pool of blood. His bicycle and a few parcels of meat lay flung to one side. The murderers were never caught. Only a faint clue as to their identity was on Old Ben's face. He had died laughing and the stab wound had been inflicted under the right armpit, down into the right lung, rupturing it. A group of young boys had accosted Old Ben the previous evening and he had had no way of knowing that they were imitating the way of life around them where the taking of human life was just as easy and natural as breathing and that these children had recently formed themselves into a gang and he was to be their first kill. He had laughed. They were all known to him. He thought they wanted pennies. And they had laughed too. No one would ever know that they had turned into monsters overnight to dominate and terrorise the future and get rich, wear smart clothes and drive big cars like their fathers. Humanity was long dead anyway. Gangsters were the heroes of the day in their environment and they were the children of rape and all forms of uncurbed brutality. And the stunned crowd of people who gathered around the body of Old Ben perhaps sensed this; that something hideous had been unleashed in their midst and would consume them all. For what had Old Ben ever done except spend a life time warming people's hearts; at least those with hearts left.

So had young Jimmy Motsisi. People got into the habit of referring to him as the ideal family man and just seeing him pass by every day warmed their hearts because there were so few good men left. His open, honest-looking face made him the kind of person people entrusted with small sums of money to purchase goods for them in town. He was liked and respected by the gangsters because he never lost his head or good humour in any situation. It was the custom of gangsters to rob hard working family men of their pay packets on Friday nights but they always overlooked Jimmy's pay packet. After all, they reasoned illogically, he had six children to feed. Yet they unblinkingly robbed men with families of twelve. The cause of this strange reasoning among the gangsters was Jimmy's exemplary conduct as a husband. He never spent money on drink and his wife was the only girl in his life.

All this was a rather glib assessment of a very complicated young man. Goodness and honesty were not hard won virtues in him but an instinctive part of a personality pattern. This personality fitted in with a book of rules presented to him by his parents who somehow failed to point out that these rules are arrived at in hit or miss fashion through the trials and errors of life and that the individual is constantly exposed to the impact of his environment and at the mercy of his own secret subterranean desires and that everything, especially rules, has a way of exploding in your face one fine day.

The funny thing is, people of the township said Daphne Matsulaka would not survive long when she first arrived. It was plain to all that she was a nice-timer and practised 'gangsters moll' and the place was riddled with real tough big-time gangsters. They expected her to be annihilated within a week in the competition that would ensue for her favour. But nothing of the kind happened. She established her own supremacy with a hard, imperious, queenly stare and everyone gave way before it. Besides, she looked as rich as ten devils, always dressed to the teeth in tight-fitting, expensive costumes and swanky high-heeled shoes. She was quite trim about the hips but swayed them in a slightly exaggerated manner and this caused her high-heeled shoes to make a loud, distinct 'clip-clop' sound as she walked. The women of the township soon nicknamed her 'The Queen of Sheba' and giggled among themselves as she passed. But they were afraid. The men just stared with fascinated expressions on their faces. But they were afraid too. They knew a walking time-bomb, only in which direction it would explode was anybody's guess. 'Hot Sparks' Phalane had already openly declared that he would shoot her dead if she chose his rival 'Big Brain' Mazooki.

The lady took her time. The little match-box house she had rented at the most southerly tip of the horse-shoe near the railway station, had to be transformed. It needed a telephone, carpets, a stereo-phonic radiogram, discreet lighting and a thousand and one odds and ends. When everything had been arranged to her satisfaction, she settled down to playing her little game. It was something like the game children play when they run through a pair of arched arms and sing:

Oranges and lemons,
Say the bells of St Clements,
I owe you a farthing,
When will you pay me,
When I grow rich . . .
Well, here comes the chopper to chop off your head . . .
Chip, chop. Chip chop,
The last man's head off!

She sat on the porch each morning in a fluffy powder-blue dressing gown and played this little game with her eyes. All the men had to pass by her house to get to the railway station nearby. They interested her as the men of her world had never had to rush for trains. They'd all had the latest model cars. Now she felt she might be missing something, after all, in this world of busy work-a-day men, and she made up her mind to explore it.

The last man to reach the railway station each morning was Jimmy. He attracted her eye for a number of reasons. He was the worst-dressed man in the crowd. He wore baggy, outdated pants and a checkered outdated coat, one size too big and he never seemed aware of his comical person. In fact, he seemed entirely unaware of his person. Sometimes he walked with his hand in one pocket, gazing anxiously at the ground. Sometimes he stared straight ahead with his eyebrows screwed up into an inverted 'v' shape. What puzzled, perplexed and absorbed him to the exclusion even of her majestic presence seated on the porch? With an experienced eye she stripped him down to his essentials. She noted the way in which he walked, the firm inward rolling movement of his feet. Only very sensuous men walked this way yet nothing in his face indicated that he was aware of his sensuousness and this excited her.

It wasn't difficult to find a woman who was hostile to his wife, Mary and from this woman she gleaned all the necessary details of his family life. The wife, Mary, was tired and over-strained from having borne children one year after another within six years of marriage. She was often snappish and cross, with the children, with neighbours with the husband. The youngest, a baby of six months, was perpetually ill and kept up a day and night wail. But all this did not disturb the husband. He spent a part of every evening nursing, feeding and soothing the troublesome infant, thus relieving Mary. Also, his eldest son, aged six had just started school and it delighted the father to listen to his son re-reading the day's lesson. Then, only after the children had been put to bed, would Jimmy devote himself to his own interest. He was very fond of reading the newspaper and this he did thoroughly and with great concentration, reading it from end to end, even the 'births and deaths' and advertisement columns. Often he'd discuss some item of interest with Mary who sat nearby quietly mending or ironing the day's washing, and really, though neither of them questioned why it was so, this was the most enjoyable part of the evening; as though a whole day had been lived through for these quiet murmured discussions about the affairs of the world which did not really concern them. Jimmy worked for a printing firm in the city and often his salary of eight pounds a week did not provide for adequate meals. Often supper was only bread and jam and tea but these quiet, peaceful endings to the day made it all strangely satisfying and worthwhile.

The lady weighed this information up very carefully. She had, after all, been missing something and this was intolerable to her pride. Besides, she had some definite advantages over the drab dull wife and she knew at sight one of his fatal weaknesses. The next morning she cleared her throat as he passed by which made Jimmy pause and stare in surprise. Too many things caught his eye all at once — the brightly coloured flowers in pots, the shiny polished porch and the frothy haze of a powder-blue dressing gown above which a pair of large black carefully mascaraed eyes stared at him boldly.

'Hul-lo', the lady said in a sweet, sugary voice. And Jimmy, after all, was like men the world over and immediately attracted and excited by cheap tinsel.

'I . . . er . . . I had no idea anyone was living here', he stuttered.

'That's because you're always searching the ground for six-pences, sweetie', she said, and giggled.

The train was approaching and he shifted restlessly but the bold black eyes hypnotised him with their awful secrets and mysteries. He had to tear himself away from the spell just as the train was about to pull out of the station.

She was there again on the porch when he returned home, this time dressed in a dazzling pink costume. He stumped his foot on a stone, feeling foolish and uncertain of himself. She smiled and said:

'Why don't you come in and have some tea?'

He thought.

'Well, I won't stay long. I have to get home and help Mary with the infant.'

The house was no different from all the box houses of the area. There was the one large room that served as a dining room and kitchen and the two tiny cramped rooms for bedrooms.

But he had never, in his wildest dreams, imagined an interior like this. It looked like a smart furniture shop with its carpets, couches, pale yellow, pink and blue walls and dim lighting. A delicate perfume pervaded the atmosphere.

'I can't stay long', Jimmy said, as he nervously seated himself on the edge of one of the couches.

'I see', the lady said thoughtfully. 'You're worried about the wife. Is she the dominating type?'

'Er . . . no', he said, surprised.

'Well then, tell her you had to work overtime', the lady said.

She placed a small table near him and into a very small glass she poured a very small amount of liquor which she handed to him. There was something lovely, soft and caressing in her every movement and gesture. Bemused, he leaned back and settled himself deeply in the soft couch.

The liquor went straight to his head almost numbing his brain and arms and legs. A backache that had afflicted him for years quietly eased itself away and the noise, the awful clamouring terrible noise of third class coaches and wailing babies dissolved into an overwhelming dark silence. He closed his eyes. Immediately, a vivid picture of Mary pacing up and down with the screaming infant flashed into view. He pushed it away from him resentfully. Noting all this, the lady smiled to herself and slipped down onto her knees before him and gently removed his shoes. She had a basin of warm water nearby into which she dropped a cube of some sweet-smelling stuff. She raised his feet and put them into the basin of water.

'What's that you put in the water?' he asked innocently.

'Oh it's just something the chemist recommended for tired feet', she said, carelessly.

'How much does it cost?' he asked.

The lady looked surprised.

'Don't you have any at home?' she said. 'Your wife ought to buy some. It only costs a shilling a cube.' Which was a lie. It had cost her twenty shillings a cube and either this indirect jibe at Mary or his sensing the lie caused a swift change of mood in him.

'I'll have to leave soon', he said and there was a slight chill in his voice.

And yet he stayed to supper. And he stayed the night. It was shock and guilt that made him foolishly rush home early the next morning before going to work. His head was so muddled, he could not really find a coherent excuse for why he had failed to come home the previous night. He stood at the door of his own home an outcast and stranger. It wasn't even his wife, this stranger with two dark smudged eyes. And all she said was:

'Tell her not to smear your cheek with lipstick.'

And after he had gone away she quietly added to herself:

'Oh God, help me.'

And God, when appealed to, has rather drastic ways of assisting the individual. He sent sympathy to an undefended woman in the shape of the gangsters and this forced Mary to remove herself and the children from the township within one week.

The lady promised to pay for the divorce on the grounds of desertion. It was known throughout the township that she and Jimmy were to marry. For a time Jimmy lived this new heavenly life of ease and comfort but after a few weeks he was unfortunately put on overtime at work. On the first day he arrived home at 10 o'clock, he found the lady in an ugly, stamping rage. He was surprised out of the clouds of tender kisses in which he had been living.

'I've been working overtime', he said truthfully.

The truth was something men of her world had never told her and this served to increase her fury.

'I suppose you think I'm Mary', she snarled. 'I'm just reminding you that this is *my* house.'

Jimmy spent a miserable night alone on one of the couches. The following day he was faced with a decision: either to lose his job or spend another night on the couch. He decided to spend another night on the couch.

When he arrived home he found the house in complete darkness. The door was locked. He knocked. There was no reply. Inside the house the lady quietly lifted the receiver off the telephone.

'Police', she whispered urgently. 'There's a trespasser outside my door. Come quickly. Oh Help! Help! My life is in danger!'

Jimmy paced up and down the porch, not comprehending this latest development. In his pacing he almost tripped over a bundle in the darkness. He struck a match and bent down. It was his belongings. The world somersaulted in that brief moment but it heaved unbelievingly when a police van screeched to a stop outside the gate and he was bodily thrown in. He never really remembered that night in the cell and the brief court hearing the following morning at which he paid a ten pound admission of guilt fee for trespassing on private property. Discordant sounds were to fill his mind forever after that. One of them was the clip-clop. Clip-clop. Clip-clop. Distinct, indignant clip and clop of the lady's high-heeled shoes as she walked up to the witness box.

Something went wrong too with a normally calm centre of his body, just near the heart. It seemed as though a storm water drain had burst, just there. There was this rushing turmoil of sound that drowned out all other sounds. It was very painful. It put the whole mechanism of his life out of gear. Sometimes it made him imagine he was furiously hungry and he'd eat anything he could get hold of. Sometimes he could not touch food for days. The management and control of this pain absorbed all his living hours, yet it was beyond control and management and greedy beyond words, sucking inwards all his attentiveness in its roar. Only brandy soothed it. Only brandy released him from the abysmal nightmare and bottles and bottles of it he drank before he died. He was never to know how a few kind friends struggled to keep him alive through that last agonising month. He never really saw their aghast, pity-stricken faces as he held an imaginary newspaper in front of him and discussed the news of the day the way he used to with Mary.

As for the lady, Daphne Matsulaka, she survived well enough. She took up with 'Big Brain' Mazooki after he had shot dead his rival, 'Hot Sparks' Phalane.

Snowball

It is Autumn in Cape Town. Each day the sunset is new, with a new theme, but the underlying mood is always the same. Always the still, chilled Autumn air controls the earth's scent with a nostalgic sweetness that is unlike any other season of the year. Sharp, and distinct, these scents blend with the yellow-gold sky as it imperceptibly changes to a powdery mauve and then a vivid, splashy orange-red that pulsates and pulsates. Two children pass by, barefoot, absorbed, with comic red-painted sunset faces. Suddenly the sharp black silhouette of rooftops appear outlined against the glowing sky.

It is strange how a scene or a street can evoke pleasant or unpleasant memories. It is strange, too, how one's life is rather like a railway station. People pass in and out all the time and yet so few are of consequence to one's destiny. If the sunset reminds me of 'Snowball' it is only because during the time I knew him I was driven by a strong urge to protect him. He was too passive and peace-loving and life knocked him around an awful lot. He merely took each blow as it came without question or thought of retaliation. I imagine the only peace he ever found was when he was at sea in his small dinghy. I imagine, too, that he was the kind of man who would notice a sunset.

Capetonians have a witty way of giving people queer nicknames. But often these nicknames make sense. Just say all the fingers of one hand may be missing, then they might call you 'Vyf' and you would not mind at all because the way in which it was said would bear a tender regard for your defect; even to the point of giving you great prestige in the neighbourhood. But the nickname 'Snowball' never really made sense to me because 'Snowball' was a man who was quite black all over except for his clean white teeth. I must admit that there are many things in Cape Town that confuse me! Strangely enough 'Snowball' did not mind being called 'Snowball' though if I had been in his place, I would have made very effort to acquire another nickname. It just would have made me hot all over to be called 'Snowball'.

I first met 'Snowball' when we moved into a crowded four-roomed house in District Six. The housing situation being what it is, my husband and I were immensely grateful to obtain a clean large room to ourselves with a bathroom and were prepared to put up with the hazardous and inexplicable behaviour of our landlord and landlady. Our landlord was forever threatening us with bodily assault, ably abetted by our landlady who alternately suffered from fits of wild generosity and wild anger. One never knew where one stood in such a storm-filled atmosphere. I myself am not usually very obliging. I loathe to be at the mercy of those who make irrational demands. But then life can teach one some very humbling lessons, as my landlady said: 'Put out the light', I put it out. If, five minutes later she said: 'Put it on', I put in on. But underneath the rebel fumed and fumed and frequently there were were sharp explosions; threats of physical violence, a lot of hot air and an electric tension which were as suddenly stilled by an outburst of wild generosity on the part of my landlady. It always overcomes me when an enemy reaches out the hand of peace. I'm terribly bad at making up.

With my husband there was never a note of discord. He is naturally tactful and a skilful negotiator of human relationships. They adored him. All in all, we, the tenants, were a subdued lot; 'Snowball' perhaps the most subdued of us all. I mean, we all had a little party now and then, took a drink and sort of let go. But 'Snowball' had forsaken all worldly pleasures. He was a convert and every evening one would see him quietly sitting in some obscure corner with his head stuck in the Bible. But it made no difference. It only goaded everyone, and my landlady in particular, into reminding him loudly that he was once a professional thief and all those bruises and scars on his face were because he had served an eight-year jail sentence. To them, 'Snowball's' religion was a cover up. A thief is always a thief. It must have taken great strength of character to stick to religion in the face of such provocation.

It is important to expand a bit on 'Snowballs' religion. He was very wide and broad-minded wherein science and spiritualism and all other contradictory ideas could live in chaotic happiness. I have immense respect for such broad-mindedness. It appears to me, from the way they talk, that many converted people severely restrict themselves to reading the Bible. Darwin is out, because he contradicts the story of Adam and Eve. Aldous Huxley is definitely out, because he once had the audacity to say that God was unnecessary. Well, before I ever came to discussing 'Snowball's' religion with him, I had a peek into his room, saw Aldous Huxley and his 'perennial Philosophy' among all those pamphlets, leaflets and paths of truth. It surely helps to introduce a lot of contradiction into religion. I think so.

The first question 'Snowball' asked me when we got to discussing things was whether I was a soul with a body or a body with a soul. Since I have many converted friends I was bound to know the answer to that one, so I answered promptly: 'I am a soul with a body.'

I was amazed at the smile of intense happiness that spread over his face. I felt like a cheat because it must have taken him and my friends many gruelling hours of thought to have arrived at any sort of answer that satisfied them. The question does not concern me either way but then I had to learn that my flippant, cynical attitude towards religion is useless. Possibly it was only a man like 'Snowball' who could give me a humbling lesson in that direction. For one thing, he was basically good and gentle. That is something that cannot be faked . . . goodness. For another, he had a curious mind that was incapable of taking a dogmatic stand. Contradiction or even apparent contradiction could be called the other name of truth. That night 'Snowball' and I discussed many things that are not even mentioned in the Bible.

I would have liked to be a strong ally and defend and protect 'Snowball' from all the harsh blows that landed on

30

his head. An impossible task! Once I tried. I heard our land-lady loudly berating him for being a dirty man. I could not see how he could be, because he was the only tenant in the house who bathed every night. I told her so, but she looked at me blankly, pretending not to hear. I never tried again. In fact, one just became accustomed to hear 'Snowball' getting it in the neck again about something or other. His crayfish had a way of lying dead for hours and then suddenly arising and walking about the house. He could hardly pay the rent because each day a well-to-do cousin seized three-quarters of the profits on the fish under the pretext that he had paid for the dinghy. Something was always happening to 'Snowball'.

One day, during a sudden high summer gale, his dinghy capsized, and I have as yet found no answer to the people who pass in and out of my life.

Sorrow food

I eat only sorrow food now. It's my way of saying that the guys who're at the winning post now won't listen to me. Figure this out. When these guys, who're the whip now, were still being nursed by their tribal grandmothers, I was in New York, getting my education. And I don't mean going to school. Ha! Ha! I came back here and got this stinking Job's country of cattle jumping with politics. Now these guys say:

'Boshwa, you're the high-powered car with the battery run flat!'

'Sure, sure', I say. 'But I'm still up for sale. We're blood brothers, playing the same dirty game — how to get rich quickly. Yeah. You guys got the edge on me. I backed a loser. I should've known Pan Africanism'd never hit this goddam tribal backwater. Now you guys have cut it smart, kissing the tribal stool. O.K. I figure I'll travel along. Load your vote. I'm in the clear. The colonial bastards can't stick the commie label on me. The colonials can make a commie a dead dog. And Boshwa doesn't care to be *that* kind of dead dog! He lives to see another day.'

Yeah. That's what I've come down to — begging sorrow food. The guys who're in, chuck it back. They figure they couldn't travel along with a guy like me. I've got good food from the colonial bastards. For their kind of game I am not a dirty commie. They say:

'That Boshwa! He's a wit. He has a sense of humour!'

And all that crap is a cover-up for their kind of game. Who's running the goddam show here — black men or white men? I tell you it's not clear. I figure I'm a black man and I figure the guys who're in are black men. You get a kind of bitter feeling at this critical stage in the history of Africa. The guys who're in hold off on me. I'm a hell of an embarrassment. Some guys like to do everything under cover of darkness. I like the clear light of day. I don't give a damn to conceal anything. I call a prostitute a prostitute and pay for

32

services rendered. Other guys don't pay. They shoot a long line — all for a free ride.

When I get a woman I say:

'Here's your five bucks. Africa is one big, loose penis female. Thanks for the ride.'

So you see — the thing between the guys who're in and myself is a purely personal consideration. They don't know what to do with an honest guy. I'm not saying I have a conscience. I'm just saying I'm honest. There's a hell of a broad space between conscience and honesty. Hell, I can get quite philosophical about this subject. I figure I'm some of the mess Africa's in today. No foothold. Skidding downhill. Booze, booze, booze. Women, women, women. A guy kind of gets it up to his neck till he could pass out. Here's two sides to the story. If you're a tribe guy, you're goddam safe. If you're a guy who's been around, this goddam tribe hits you like a myth. Stone age history. The first guy wants to sit on it he feels so safe. What's the other guy to do? Take a guy like me, for instance. If I'm busting out it's from necessity. Stress. Breaking point. Take a tribe guy. If he's busting out, it's for his afternoon exercise! Change? It's a thing he can't comprehend in this critical stage of the history of Africa. Give him his lolly, his female, his booze, and he's a well-fed guy with no complaints. The pip-arsed white man's going to stick around in Southern Africa until either God or the commies bust the show!

High-powered car. Ha! Ha! I'm no high-powered car. I'm an ignition key, starter. The kind of guy who can't stand the rut. Yeah. I'm the guy who goes places. Only I have the Midas touch. Everything turns to stone. I've had a nodding acquaintance with every goddam bastard. I was famous. I was tough. But every goddam thing in me turns to stone. You know what's fire from heaven? Maybe you don't. It has to be seen to be believed. I used to be familiar with the old man upstairs. I used to be a lay preacher. Folks used to say I could bring that old man down from there and tell him what he ought to do. Then the guy began to get me:

'Either me or the females and the booze.'

I said:

'No dice. The females and the booze.'

I used to have a touch with females but that's turned to stone too. What's a guy to do after New York? After he's knocked around in Harlem and seen real female legs in high-stepping shoes? Take the tribe females. Dress almost down to ankle length. Scarf covering the head up to the eyes. Goddam! I like a pretty female, painted up. Bright yellow, green, red, pink dress with the knees showing. The only kind of female who'd do that here is a hard-flint flossie. They're in-between women till our women begin to catch up with this critical stage in the development of Africa.

After I'd parted company with the old man upstairs, I tried politics. The thing I like about politics is that it's such a dirty game any bastard can play. It's a kind of game I have stamina for. Sure I backed a loser, but I'd still make a good opposition. So I'm sticking around.

You know. In Africa you always know what's coming to you. Ask the old men. They're the spokesmen of the nation. There was that solemn, plodding old tribal wit. He'd been at every meeting I'd spoken at — just sitting and listening. Then one day he creaked up on his old bones and raised his hand — commandingly. When that old bugger stood up like that I knew the judgement day had come. Whatever he said was going to fix things in his village, in his third uncle's village, and so on.

So I just ignored the bugger.

I said:

'Vasco Da Gama said he discovered the Cape, but when he got there the black man was already there. Ha! Ha!'

It always raises a laugh, even though I've said it one thousand goddam times. The old bugger stood there pointedly and the rock of ages didn't laugh. Soon the crowd began looking enquiringly at this rock.

They said:

'Sit down, old man. It's not time for questions.'

But the old bugger would not. Now, I'm a democratic guy. Thanks to New York. I'm a democratic guy — at my ease. I'm a cosmopolitan guy — at my ease. The old bastard wouldn't have done it with a tribe guy but he didn't click with me. Anyway, I like a show-down.

So I said:

'What is it, old father?'

He said:

'I have a proposition to make to you.' (For christ's sake!)

I said:

'We're listening, old father.'

He pulled up the kind of voice to shake the devil. My father used to do the same before he whipped me. It's an old, old African trick.

He said:

'Sir, with all respects, we do not see how we can vote for you.'

I said:

'Ha! Ha! Explain yourself, old father.'

The old bugger raised his hand, — another old African trick to frighten the devil.

He said:

'How can we vote for you. I would not trust you to bank five pounds of my money. How can we trust the vote to you?'

'Ha! Ha!' I do it out of habit. Life's a bloody joke.

'Laughter is inappropriate', he said severely. 'My relative in Mabelapudi last year contributed twenty pounds as a donation when you came in great anxiety to say your wife needed an operation for polio. Soon we saw your wife walking about quite fresh in good health. Soon we saw you had a new car. Swear unto me that it's not true!'

The bloody old hypocrite! Robbery's been sanctioned by our ancestors, only you must make like its done under cover of darkness. You must make like a chief. You want all the cattle and the cars and the females. You want to get fat, but you must rob the poor under-cover style. As I told you, I'm an honest guy. I believe in day-light robbery. Anyway, I knew I was through; the only goddam representative of Pan-Africanism at this critical stage in a goddam Job's country.

Still, a guy must defend his dignity. I mean he must defend something, especially when everybody's embarrassed. Some of the folks like me. I make them laugh. And in any case it's better when the world's a bloody mess.

So I said:

'Respectful old father, this is a political meeting — not a village council. You may pronounce judgement there.'

'Kibone', he said. In other words meaning we-have-seen-through-you.

The crowd backed me for old time's sake. They said:

'Sit down! Sit down! You heard what he said. This is a political meeting! You don't understand politics!'

They like to rub it in — to make sure you've heard, these old bastards.

'Lefirefire', he said. Meaning — rogue, thief.

The crowd said:

'Sit down! Have respect! This man is our politician. That's no way to speak to a politician!' and amid shouts the old bones creaked down.

He'll never forget it. He's crowing somewhere. He most probably thinks he's made the most original statement of the century. His goddam uncles, cousins, fourth grandmothers probably think so too. But they cannot see the subtleties. To be or not to be — a day-light robber, or an under-cover robber? There's some folks beginning to like a day-light robber. Besides it's going to take a hell of a revolution to make politics a clean game. So, while the old man up there figures out the revolution, I'm going to stick around in politics as the only representative of Pan-Africanism in this critical stage in the development of Africa. Ha! Ha!!

Chibuku Beer and Independence

The rumour went about that Rhodesia was sending tank-loads of free Chibuku beer for the Independence celebrations. To taste Chibuku beer again was almost like news from home for six young students and refugees in Francistown. They had fled from the university during the upheavals and detentions that accompanied UDI. They were eager to attend the celebrations and I went along too with my water bucket. The whole afternoon it was continuously over-flowing with Chibuku beer. We formed a tight circle in a shed and were as nasty as possible to strangers who begged a drink. Everyone had pretty pink plastic throw-away mugs and at the beer tank the law of the jungle prevailed, the stronger shoving the weaker. We prided ourselves that we drank in peace and comfort.

There was just a raggle-taggle crowd of poor people wandering about aimlessly and uncertainly.

'They call this Independence', one of the students said scornfully. 'Where's the excitement? Where's the fever?'

There were a lot more disparaging remarks.

'You should have been here at midnight', someone said. 'The British flag was lowered in dead silence. Only one voice said hooray and everyone turned around to stare at the man in surprise. I was so furious I shouted: "burn it." Can you imagine my amazement? An old man standing next to me said I should not say such things. He said I am embarrassing everyone, especially the white people present.'

Everyone laughed because the people of Botswana really baffled them. It's as though you are thoroughly astonished to find yourself at the dead calm centre of a storm that rages over the whole of Southern Africa. You never quite get used to it if you have fled the whole night and day through wild country expecting at any moment to feel a police bullet whistling through your back. And the students had that air about them — keyed-up, wild, excitable, feverish. They burst out singing the sad, defiant anthem of Southern Africa and raised their hands to the Botswana flag. 'Africa is Ours', they sang. And they kept repeating the anthem for half an hour. This drew a fascinated crowd that stood around silently, inspecting us minutely as though we were zoo animals.

We also sang:

'How many years does it take for a man to be free? —
. . . The answer is blowing in the wind . . .'

This depressed everyone and we sat in glum silence a few moments. An old man was sitting nearby. He had a perpetual smile on his wizened old face. He had walked many miles from the bush to celebrate independence. The skin on his knees was deeply creased and abnormally stretched from having spent most of his life in a squatting position. He looked at us with his beautiful smile and said in a touching childlike way: 'I like Francistown.'

Oddly, this aroused the students from their depression. They started to abuse everyone and everything again.

'You're drunk old papa', they said.

'Who, just who in this silly country knows what independence means? Just ask any one of these silly people.'

'Just look at that plain, ugly flag . . .'

'No, no', I cut in sharply, suddenly aroused too. 'The flag is very beautiful. For one thing it is a flag for everyone, above party politics. For another it is truly symbolic of the country. One broad blue stripe represents the blue sky of Botswana; the other, the people's hope for rain to develop industry and agriculture. The black and white stripes represent the ideal of racial harmony.'

They were a trifle disconcerted and looked at the flag again.

'All right', someone said. 'I only like it when it's not blowing out full in the wind. I just like that broad stripe of black in the middle.'

Someone said something about the demerits of Seretse as an African politician. Then looked at me for I have lived in Botswana for almost three years.

'There's nothing wrong with the man', I said mildly.

'What do you mean? Give us facts. Is he really an African nationalist?' they asked critically, unbelievingly.

I felt desperately uncomfortable being a non-supporter of politicians.

'He says sensible things', I said, helplessly. 'I mean, the government is quiet and when it says something one examines it closely to see if there is any evil in the statement but you can't find it. You think perhaps it might be sensible then.'

'But is the man an African nationalist?' they asked.

'Yes', I said. 'After a time I summed him up that way.'

Someone said: 'Actually, I can agree with her. I like a quiet man who shuts his mouth up when faced with a hopeless situation. Seretse is a much better politician than Dr Banda of Malawi for instance. That man makes statements all the time and they are often detrimental to African interests.'

Our party broke up in a sudden, shocking and hilarious manner. We sent one of the students, a quiet, timid fellow to re-fill the bucket at the beer tank. Just as it was full he looked up into the sharp edge of a knife.

'Give it', a drunken voice commanded. He hastily surrendered the bucket. Then the whole drunken crew of men about the tank fell upon the bucket with wild abandon and pulled it from end to end bathing their heads in beer. This was too much for the students. They flew into the fray, their arms in the air like wild birds. A Botswana policeman calmly intervened and tippled the remaining contents of the beer on the ground. The students ground their teeth in frustrated fury.

'These Botswana police are silly', they said. 'We could have made a coup on that bucket without any bloodshed.'

I walked home alone. There was the ever-familiar thorn bush lit up by the brilliant fierce beauty of a desert sunset. Only a new unfamiliar feature; the blue, black and white flag straining in the strong breeze.

'It is all right', I thought. 'The whole world seems topsy-turvy but there is a something here in this country that is good. Perhaps it is a weird kind of people who pull against the current; unprovokable; even reasonable. Perhaps it is the rags and tatters of poverty that are worn with an upright posture and pathetic dignity. What ever it is I say it is good because you feel it in your heart as peace.'

Village People

Poverty has a home in Africa — like a quiet second skin. It may be the only place on earth where it is worn with an unconscious dignity. People do not look down at your shoes which are caked with years of mud and split so that the toes stick out. They look straight and deeply into your eyes to see if you are friend or foe. That is all that matters. To some extent I think that this eye-looking, this intense human awareness, is a reflection of the earth all about. There is no end to African sky and to African land. One might say that in its vastness is a certain kind of watchfulness that strips man down to his simplest form. If that is not so, then there must be some other, unfathomable reason for the immense humanity and the extreme gentleness of the people of my village.

Poverty here has majority backing. Our lives are completely adapted to it. Each day we eat a porridge of millet in the morning; a thicker millet porridge with a piece of boiled meat at midday; and at evening we repeat breakfast. We use our heads to transport almost everything: water from miles and miles, bags of corn and maize, and fire wood.

This adaptation to difficult conditions in a permanently drought-stricken country is full of calamity. Babies die most easily of starvation and malnutrition: and yet, within this pattern of adaptation people crowd in about the mother and sit, sit in heavy silence, absorbing the pain, till, to the mother, it is only a dim, dull ache folded into the stream of life. It is not right. There is a terrible mindlessness about it. But what alternative? To step out of this mindless safety, and face the pain of life alone when the balance is heavily weighted down on one side, is for certain to face a fate far worse. Those few who have, are insane in a strange, quiet, harmless way: walking all about the village, freely. Only by their ceaseless muttering and half-clothed bodies are they distinguishable from others. It is not right, as it is negative merely to strive for existence. There must be other ingredients boiling

41

in the pot. Yet how? We are in the middle of nowhere. Most communication is by ox cart or sledge. Poverty also creates strong currents of fear and anxiety. We are not outgoing. We tend to push aside all new intrusions. We live and survive by making as few demands as possible. Yet, under the deceptive peace around us we are more easily confused and torn apart than those with the capacity to take in their stride the width and the reach of new horizons.

Do we really retain the right to develop slowly, admitting change only in so far as it keeps pace with our limitations, or does change descend upon us as a calamity? I merely ask this because, anonymous as we are, in our favour is a great credit balance of love and warmth that the Gods somewhere should count up. It may be that they overlook desert and semi-desert places. I should like to remind them that there are people here too who need taking care of.

The old woman

She was so frail that her whole body swayed this way and that like a thin stalk of corn in the wind. Her arms were as flat as boards. The flesh hung loosely, and her hands which clutched the walking stick were turned outwards and knobbled with age. Under her long dress also swayed the tattered edges of several petticoats. The ends of two bony stick-legs peeped out. She had on a pair of sand-shoes. The toes were all sticking out, so that the feet flapped about in them. She wore each shoe on the wrong foot, so that it made the heart turn over with amusement.

Yet she seemed so strong that it was a shock when she suddenly bent double, retched and coughed emptily, and crumbled to the ground like a quiet sigh.

'What is it, Mmm? What is the matter?' I asked.

'Water, water.' she said faintly.

'Wait a minute. I shall ask at this hut here if there is any water.'

'What is the matter?' they asked.

'The old lady is ill.' I said.

'No.' she said curtly. 'I am not ill. I am hungry.'

The crowd laughed in embarrassment that she should display her need so nakedly. They turned away, but old ladies have no more shame left. They are like children. They give way to weakness and cry openly when they are hungry.

'Never mind.' I said. Hunger is a terrible thing. My hut is not far away. This small child will take you. Wait till I come back, then I shall prepare food for you.'

Then, it was late afternoon. The old lady had long passed from my mind when a strange young woman, unknown to me, walked into the yard with a pail of water on her head. She set it down outside the door and squatted low.

'Good-day. How are you?' I said.

She returned the greeting, keeping her face empty and carefully averted. It is impossible to say: what do you want? Whom are you looking for? It is impossible to say this to a carefully averted face and a body that squats quietly, patiently. I looked at the sky, helplessly. I looked at the trees. I looked at the ground, but the young woman said nothing. I did not know her, inside or out. Many people I do not know who know me, inside and out, and always it is this way, this silence.

A curious neighbour looked over the hedge.

'What's the matter?' she asked.

I turned my eyes to the sky again, shrugging helplessly.

'Please ask the young woman what she wants, whom she is looking for.'

The young woman turned her face to the neighbour, still keeping it averted, and said quietly:

'No, tell her she helped our relative who collapsed this morning. Tell her the relatives discussed the matter. Tell her we had nothing to give in return, only that one relative said she passes by every day on her way to the water tap. Then we decided to give a pail of water. It is all we have.'

Tell them too. Tell them how natural, sensible, normal is human kindness. Tell them, those who judge my country, Africa, by gain and greed, that the gods walk about her barefoot with no ermine and gold-studded cloaks.

All day long I lie asleep under the thorn tree, and the desert is on this side of me and on that side of me. I have no work to do. We are all waiting for the rain, as we cannot plough without rain. I think the rain has gone away again, like last year. We had a little rain in November, but December has gone, and now it is January; and each day we have been sitting here, waiting for rain: my mother, my grandmother and my grandfather, my cousin Lebenah, and my sister and her little baby. If it were to rain my grandfather would push the plough and my cousin Lebenah would pull the oxen across the great miles of our land. We women would follow behind, sowing maize, millet, pumpkin and watermelon seed. I feel great pity for my family, and other families. I wonder why we sit here like this. Each day the sun is hot, hot in the blue sky. Each day the water pool of November rain gets smaller. Soon we will have to leave the land and return to the village.

In the village we have a politician who takes the people up on the hill to pray for rain. He wears a smart suit and has a big black car and a beautiful deep African voice. His mind is quick and moves from one thing to another. He can pray, and cry, and speak politics all at once. People always expect the rain to fall the minute after he has stopped praying and crying. They call him the one who has shaken God loose.

Actually, I have not been sleeping the whole day. I am trying to learn English. My cousin Lebenah tells me that things are changing in Africa, and that it is necessary for women to improve themselves. I love my cousin Lebenah so much that I do anything he tells me to do. He tells me that English is the best language to learn, as many books have been written in English, and that there is no end to the knowledge that can be gained from them. He gave me a geography book and I have read it over and over. I am puzzled and afraid. Each year the sun is more cruel. Each year the rain becomes less and less. Each year more and more of our cattle die. The only animal that survives is the goat. It can eat anything and we eat the goat. Without the goat, I do not know what we would do. It is all about us, like the family. It has the strangest eyes. They are big and yellow, and the pupil is a black streak right across the yellow ball of the eye.

I am trying to improve myself too, as I am very afraid that I may have an illegitimate baby like my elder sister. My family will suffer much. And the child too. It may die. There is never enough food and we are always hungry. It is not so easy for a woman to have too many babies when she has improved her mind. She has to think about how she will feed the baby, clothe it, and wash it. My sister's baby is lovely, though. He laughs a lot for no reason at all.

My geography book makes me wonder and wonder. It tells me that water is formed by hydrogen and oxygen. I wonder so much about that. If we had green things everywhere, they might help to make the oxygen to make the rain. The soil is very fertile. If there is only a little rain, green things come out everywhere, and many strange flowers. How can we live like this? Here are our bags with the seeds of maize, and millet, and the land is hard as stone.

Tomorrow the sun will rise, quietly. The many birds in the bush will welcome it. I do not. Alone, without the help of rain it is cruel, killing and killing. All day we look on it, like on death. Then, at evening, all is as gentle as we are. Mother roasts goat meat over the coals of the wood fire. Sister feeds her baby. Grandfather and cousin Lebenah talk quietly to each other about little things. The stars spread across the sky and bend down at the horizon. The quiet talk of grandfather and cousin Lebenah seem to make earth and heaven come together. I do not know what we would do if we all did not love one another, because tomorrow the sun will rise again.

The green tree

This small hill of my village in Africa abounds with the song of birds. The birds are small and brown and seem bound up in the thick profusion of dark brown branches. The green leaves of the trees are so minute that the eye can hardly see them. Everything that is green in my country is minute and cramped, for my country is semi-desert.

From this hill you may think the village below a fertile valley. It is shrouded and hidden in tall greenery. But that greenery is unproductive, contained and drawn into itself, concerned alone with its silent fight for survival. We call it the green tree. It came here as a stranger and quickly adapted itself to the hardness of our life. It needs no water in the earth but draws into itself the moisture of the air for its life. We use it as a hedge. It also protects us from the sandstorms that blow across our desolate and barren land.

If you tell my people that there are countries with hills and hills of green grass where no cattle graze, they will not believe you. Our cattle graze on parched grass that is paper-dry. Our goats eat the torn shreds of wind-scattered papers and thrust their mouths into the thorn bushes to nibble at the packed cluster of leaves that look like pin-points of stars farflung in the heavens. That is our life. Everything is jealously guarded. Nothing is ever given out. All strength and energy must be contained for the fight to survive tomorrow and tomorrow and tomorrow.

Many strangers traverse our land these days. They are fugitives from the south fleeing political oppression. They look on our lives with horror and quickly make means to pass on to the paradise of the north. Those who are pressed by circumstances and forced to tarry a while, grumble and complain endlessly. It is just good for them that we are inbred with habits of courtesy, hospitality and kindness. It is good that they do not know the passion we feel for this we love which cannot be touched by them. The powdery dust of the earth, the heat, the cattle with their slow, proud walk — all this has fashioned our way of life. Our women with their tall thin hard bodies can drive a man to the depth of passion. All this is ours. Few are they, strangers, who like the green tree are quickly able to adapt themselves to our way of life. They are to be most feared for the adaptation is merely on the surface, like a mask, while underneath they are new and as strange as ever. They cause a ripple on the smooth pond of life that cannot be stopped from spreading from one thing to another.

None can be more sure of this than I. For thirty-eight

years of my life I have lived in full control of myself. Now, I am full of conflict due to unaccustomed feelings that have taken possession of me. I am weakened and confused and no longer recognise myself as the man I once was. I am at one moment enraged to the point of blind destruction and the next overcome by a terrifying and utterly foreign feeling of tenderness.

With women a man must be direct, blunt, and brutal. If not, he soon finds that he loses his pride and becomes dependent on her. It is not necessary to control the passions but it is necessary to be in full control of the heart.

This strange obsession crept in on my life unaware. I do not know where I first saw her. I have not even spoken to her but now my eyes seek her out in every corner of the village and I am pursued by a thousand devils of restlessness if I do not see her. Deceitful stranger, she has put on the mask of adaptability and assumed our ways and manners but to her, the woman, all gates are closed. It is just as well that she fears me. Sometimes I could destroy her with the thunderbolt of violence that is within me and I see the shock and terror reflected in her eyes. Then, when I am not able to control the feelings that obsess me, it is I in turn who tremble at her sharp daring look of gloating power and indifference. It is I who stand unmanned, drained of strength and will and my rage and hatred at the loss of my pride and independence drive me beyond the bounds of sanity.

Everything I have wanted I have had through force, cunning or calculation. Now, I lie awake at night, craving something I fear to possess. Just as our cattle would go insane at the unaccustomed sight of a hill covered with greenery; so do I live in fear of the body of a woman that has been transplanted by upheaval and uncertain conditions into harsh and barren soil. Sometimes I feel it beneath me; cool, like the depths of the night when the moon brings the pale light of heaven to earth and makes the dust shimmer like gold. Then my hands reach out to crush the life out of the thing that torments me.

A desert has a strange effect on human life. As long as you search for outward things like underground water and possible new grazing ground for your cattle, all is well. But should an inward longing awaken in you then your life becomes very unsafe. There is no possible way of fulfilling these longings when the fight for survival is so intense. We desert people are in some way cruel. We are too much like the starkness and desolation that surround us. Sometimes you cannot tell where man ends and nature begins. The pattern of his hard, gnarled brown body is repeated in the pattern of the hard, dry, dark and leafless trees. We are a complement to the earth. Nature is extreme and violent. We are gentle and conciliatory as though making up to her for the mercifulness she lacks. We tolerate no violent eruptions of feeling; no quarrelling. Any dispute between neighbour and neighbour, husband and wife is thoroughly and openly discussed in the village courts. We are passionately addicted to long speeches and in that way rid ourselves of all passion. Really, I do not think we understand the inward life at all. We are always suppressing it. The weight of group thinking and group feeling always suppresses individual thought and initiative. In that way it is hard to change us. Our country is the poorest on the continent of Africa and at least five hundred centuries behind the rest of the world. Even our political independence is a reflection of our life. It moves against the trend of politics in Africa. People in the North, who won their independence with prison terms, blood and tears, find us very amusing.

'Where have you ever heard of an African government defending British imperialism', they say.

'But we are not like you', we say. 'We were never subjects under colonialism. We were protected people. Our fathers and grandfathers . . .' and then we make a long speech justifying ourselves.

The political refugees and busy men of these days look at us aghast.

'Don't you people know there is a war on? Don't you know about the Great White Conspiracy? They want to use this country as a buffer to stem the tide of African nationalism that is sweeping the continent! You people are playing into the hands of the settler governments! This place is dynamite! It's going to blow up sky high! You're all sitting on a keg of dynamite!'

'A keg of dynamite?'

'Just you wait and see', they hint darkly. 'You people think a tide doesn't reach a backwater?'

We defend ourselves. We make a long speech about how our country has always been peaceful and a refuge for those in trouble. We tell them the ancient story about the Kalanga tribe who fled from the persecution of the Matabele tribe and for three centuries have lived in peace here, though being a different nation with different customs.

'There is only peace here', we say, spreading our hands, eloquently.

Somehow we will never grasp the meaning of the word intrigue. Somehow we will never grasp the meaning of any of the dark torments and anxieties that ravage the human soul. All that is suppressed so deep within us that it would take an upheaval of gigantic proportions to release it. Maybe that is our greatest weakness. We who are so careful, conservative and conformist find ourselves the non-conformists of Africa. We who have only looked at life in straight lines find that there are twistings and turnings about which we know nothing. Thus, we are vulnerable and open to everything. The old people who judge everything are already uneasy.

'Miracles are happening these days', they say, unhappily.

For all the peace here we really live very unsettled lives. Desert people are migratory people. At very little provocation a whole village of cousins, aunts, parents, children will move off with goats, sheep, cattle and all; overnight. A teacher who had a class of sixty on one day finds she has no class to teach. School buildings are makeshift and equipment almost nil. Teachers never know where they will be the next day, the next term. They are always migrating after the children. In the very large villages and small towns, life is more permanent and settled so that teachers are unashamedly happy if by hook, crook or good luck they can be transferred to the towns and large villages. A large number of my teaching years had been spent drifting from one remote bush outpost to another where all that could be seen by day were the sand dunes and the rough grey stubble of the thorn trees; and at night, the stars hanging large, low and glowing in a deathly silence; so silent that it melts into the hollow cavities of loneliness, making tolerable and bearable all the unfulfilled longings. It seemed impossible that I should ever leave it, that I should be transferred to a place with a different pace of life, with a few shops, a cinema and cars tearing up and down the dusty roads the day long. Cars fascinate me. They are a strange contrast to the unchanging desert. They are shocking and defiant and new. The people who drive them are shocking and defiant and new too and hide behind dark sunglasses. It seems as though they see everything and yet their faces are remote, impassive.

The principal, for some reason a much harassed man, who spoke and walked in a jerky manner said: 'Look, there's no accommodation for teachers. You'd better see one of the officials. I don't know why they keep sending me teachers who have no relatives here.'

You never bother about accommodation. I have slept many nights in the open veld and watched the stars whirl, tumble and explode above me.

Some people are a great trouble to themselves. They are overpossessed by violent extremes of feeling that allow them no rest but drive them on endlessly, restlessly. More than others, they draw down the anger, hatred, envy and outrage of their fellow-men upon their heads. Oppose me and I'll knock you down at all costs, their fierce intent expressions seem to say. Such a man is so rare among my people that I gazed at the official to whom I had come to apply for accommodation with a startled curiosity. He looked up as I entered and right through me with blind eyes. I might have been the wall — which was also very rare. Our men have a facile kind of charm and they delight in turning it on whenever a woman appears, making some idiotic, playfully provocative joke. His face was grim and set and closed with many harsh lines etched by pain, sorrow, rage, excesses and abuses.

'I'm looking for accommodation', I said mildly, pretending I did not see all these things.

He stood up. It was effortless the way in which he held his body upright. His arms were short, powerful in strange contrast to his long, thin, slender, supple fingers. Altogether too many extremes. It seemed impossible that such an intensely masculine man should be so entirely unaware of it!

He hid his face behind the dark sunglasses and drove at tearing speed amid the twisting, dusty circular paths of the village. Goats scattered in all directions, outrage in their yellow gleaming eyes. I wish I could ride in a car like that every day. It is a wonderful feeling yet I do not know how to adequately explain it. The car stopped abruptly before one of the numerous, anonymous mud huts that seem to grow up out of and cling squatly and pathetically to the earth. A tall woman with twinkling, mischievous eyes darted out. He smiled briefly and it was like a flash of lightning across a dark and brooding sky.

'My God, Kate', he said. 'Are you still alive?'

'Of course I am, Tao', she replied with cheeky gaiety. 'I don't know why you think I should be dead when you're far older than me. Don't tell me this woman will have to stay with me. Women never live peacefully together. It looks as though I shall have to share my supper with her too. Why don't you people give us teachers increased salaries? We are such a necessary commodity but we have to live on a wage that's an old age pension.'

He smiled, again briefly.

'All you ever think about is food and money. You know things happen too slowly here.'

Then, he turned abruptly and drove off churning up the dust of the road like a furious windstorm.

'He is a strange man', I said, breaking the momentary silence between the tall woman and myself.

She shook her head.

'No, he is quite simple', she said. 'We used to play together when young. Now he is unhappy because he has a wife who loves him more than necessary; who turns the lock on the door as soon as he gets home. It offends us because she has to march about the whole village saying 'He is my husband, dark or blue.'

'Is that so?'

'Yes. Then he became a speaker for the political party and everybody says he preaches politics like a mad man. It is the straw the drowning man clutches. What may be your name, madame?'

'Lorato', I said.

'You're much of a dignity mistress but never mind, we shall be friends.'

Between the few who have and the majority who have not is a great gulf fixed. The few who have become the thing they have till man can no longer separate himself from his possessions. Without them he would be a shaken, frail, shrunken, lifeless skeleton for he has put all of himself into his possessions. To have and yet not to lose the self in the possessions; to know that there is no possibility of fulfilment of the insatiable cravings of the human soul is to know that the life of man is an ever-expanding horizon. Those who seek to constrict that horizon to possessions and things condemn themselves to a living death and a dread emptiness. The laughter and gaiety of the poor are because for them life is an expanding horizon of unattained and seemingly unattainable desires. Blessed are the poor, for they do inherit the earth.

Women of my country are faced with a strange dilemma. It is hard to see how the situation can change. Men do not feel called upon to love one particular woman; to make use of feeling. They drift from woman to woman in a carefree migratory fashion dispensing a gay, superficial, facile charm in all directions. The depths of human feeling and tenderness are never explored. Let us have a good time, they seem to say. I am here today and gone tomorrow. Therefore you have a choice. Few women choose to marry. It needs a certain amount of ruthlessness to cajole or force a man into marriage. Thereafter he has to be fiercely hoarded, not someone to love, but an object to possess, like a stack of money, a piece of furniture. Most women are repelled at the thought and never marry, though they have large families of seven or eight fatherless children and struggle to raise them on a pittance of money they gather here and there. Among the unmarried women are great and strong friendships free of jealousy and envy. No unmarried woman is ever a friend of a married woman. The great gulf is fixed. Things were different long ago when marriages were arranged by parents and elders of the village, but custom and tradition were broken down by taxation and the resultant enforced labour on the mines many miles away from home. Family life and a home are things of the past and for the future there is only continued uncertainty. With all, feeling is suppressed and put to sleep. It cannot remain so forever. Under all the gaiety and carefree laughter is a sob and it would need only a small spark to bring the emotional life to the surface, into the glare of the daylight. It is not of man's choosing but the pattern of life. Man may sleep for just so long then he must awaken to pain, heartbreak, the struggles of ambition, power, achievement.

Kate had a boyfriend; an ephemeral fly-by-night. When he came I would take a walk to the end of the village so that they might have some privacy. That was how I came upon the political meetings held at sunset under a tree on an open patch of land outside the village. A large crowd of people sat on the ground listening intently. In a van with a loudspeaker sat the man, Tao. Drawn by curiosity I joined the edge of the crowd and was immediately caught and captivated by a magnetic spell; lost to myself, while the darkness gathered all round. He could have said anything to us, that the sky was green and cows had six legs and we would have had no resistance to his persuasions. The heavy, deep, rich voice with fine, precise enunciation projected all the force, power and emotional intensity of the man; and yet a withdrawnness, an aloofness that seemed to say – You see, I have power to do as I like with you but I cannot because I respect you too much. It was that which created the strong current of trust between the man and his audience and allowed him to take them along with him, unresistingly. He was an artist, using words and plain statistics to project his own inner turmoil making earth and heaven, destiny and independence vivid and real and alive because they are all bound up in the life of man.

Any politician can tell you that the country has been prospected and certain areas found suitable for the cultivation of timber and certain areas are to be protected from animal grazing for the cultivation of crops; but few can make plain fact quiver with life. Few have such a powerful creative intelligence. A man, vividly, passionately alive, awakens all life around him. Strange that he should be one of us and yet a contrast, a new thing, the awakener of deep, hidden suppressed feeling. Such a man, with evil intentions, could cause wreckage and disaster all around him.

I walked home stunned. The whole world had become silent. I could not explain it. Also I could not explain the sudden violent pounding of the heart. Terror-stricken I wished to efface myself for fear that I am alone like the wild animal in the dark of night whose cries go unheeded because its pain is not comprehended. There is an urge to come alive yet an unwillingness to bear the pain of unfulfilment. There is humility too and a child-like need to cling to the blind earth for comfort and protection.

Kate's boyfriend had already left. She was busy cooking her evening porridge but looked up at me sharply and suspiciously. To Kate a woman's primary occupation was sleeping with a man. She was always doing it yet it horrified her moralistic soul. As I seemed unable or unwilling to attract men she had impulsively set me up on a pedestal of virtue. It made her snoop and sniff all the time as though I were hiding a man somewhere!

'Why are you so late? Where have you been?' she demanded.

I told her about the meeting and she plunged into a vigorous tirade against our politics.

'It doesn't make sense', she said. 'It's all nonsense. These two parties are shouting at each other all the time. The one says the other is right of the right and that's supposed to be a bad thing. The other is left of the left and that's supposed to be a bad thing. The people are such fools. They've already decided to support the party of the chiefs. We've been ruled for donkey's generations by the chiefs and we want to chuck them out. Instead we are all running to support the party of the rich.'

'They have a good speaker. No one can resist him.'

'I'll tell you something. It's just luck the party of the rich got him. Tao has been the poorest of the poor and now he is the richest of the rich. But the poor don't see him like that. They say he is the prophet come out of darkness to lead them to the light. The party of the rich would get nowhere without him. They sit in their houses the whole day. It's Tao all the time who speaks to us. They say he has to just address a crowd of people once and they can't run fast enough to join the party.'

'Who are you going to vote for?' I asked.

'The party of the rich', she said slyly.

'Then why do you privately favour the party of the poor?'

'A person must have two minds. If the rich think we are going to support them like blind sheep they will sit on our heads. Who may you be voting for?'

'I am not going to vote. I cannot decide matters clearly. Why do you think Tao is such a good speaker?'

'Because he is a simple man. He speaks straight from the heart. Tao is a man whose life is on display in public all the time. He can't hide anything. That is why people trust him so much.'

One night after a little rain has fallen, you awaken to find the earth covered with tender green things. And then, in the heat of the day they die or fall asleep in the parched earth to await the time when life and growth will be theirs again. They wait patiently. But the life force in man is too powerful. It makes the world tumble and fall to pieces about him. I have no courage in this upside-down world. I flee. I would rather efface myself than face the torment of a naked and unashamed desire for an unattainable man with the face of a brooding thundercloud. So, here I drift again in the remote hush and the silence. But the intensities awakened can never be put to sleep again and a spark from any direction can turn the smouldering fire within into a great conflagration.

The Woman from America

This woman from America married a man of our village and left her country to come and live with him here. She descended on us like an avalanche. People are divided into two camps. Those who feel a fascinated love and those who fear a new thing. The terrible thing is that those who fear are always in the majority. This woman and her husband and children have to be sufficient to themselves because everything they do is not the way people here do it. Most terrible of all is the fact that they really love each other and the husband effortlessly and naturally keeps his eyes on his wife alone. In this achievement he is 70 years ahead of all the men here.

We are such a lot of queer people in the southern part of Africa. We have felt all forms of suppression and are subdued. We lack the vitality, the push, the devil-may-care temperament of the people of the north of Africa. They do things first, then we. We are always going to be confederators and not initiators. We are very materialistically minded and I think this adds to our fear. People who hoard little bits of things cannot throw out and expand, and, in doing so, keep in circulation a flowing current of wealth. Basically we are mean, selfish. We eat each other all the time and God help poor Botswana at the bottom.

Then, into this narrow, constricted world came the woman from America. Some people keep hoping she will go away one day, but already her big strong stride has worn the pathways of the village flat. She is everywhere about because she is a woman, resolved and unshakeable in herself. To make matters more disturbing, she comes from the West of America, somewhere near California. I gather from her conversation that people from the West are stranger than most people. They must be the most oddly beautiful people in the world; at least this woman from the West is the most oddly beautiful person I have ever seen. Every cross-current of the earth seems to have stopped in her and blended into an amazing harmony. She has a big dash of Africa, a dash of Germany, some Cherokee and heaven knows what else. Her feet are big and her body is as tall and straight and strong as a mountain tree. Her neck curves up high and her thick black hair cascades down her back like a wild and tormented stream. I cannot understand her eyes, though, except that they are big, black and startled like those of a wild free buck racing against the wind. Often they cloud over with a deep, brooding look.

It took a great deal of courage to become friends with a woman like that. Like everyone here I am timid and subdued. Authority, everything can subdue me. Not because I like it that way but because authority carries the weight of an age pressing down on life. It is terrible then to associate with a person who can shout authority down. Her shouting-matches with authority are the terror and sensation of the village. It has come down to this. Either the woman is unreasonable or authority is unreasonable, and everyone in his heart would like to admit that authority is unreasonable. In reality, the rule is: if authority does not like you then you are the outcast and humanity associates with you at its peril. So try always to be on the right side of authority, for the sake of peace.

It was inevitable though that this woman and I should be friends. I have an overwhelming curiosity that I cannot keep within bounds. I passed by the house for almost a month, but one cannot crash in on people. Then one day a dog they have had puppies and my small son chased one of the puppies into the yard and I chased after him. Then one of the puppies became his and there had to be discussions about the puppy, the desert heat and the state of the world, and as a result of curiosity an avalanche of wealth has descended on my life. My small hut-house is full of short notes written in a wide sprawling hand. I have kept them all because they are a statement of human generosity and the wide carefree laugh of a woman who is as busy as women the world over about things women always entangle themselves in — a man, children, a home. Like this:

Have you an onion to spare? It's very quiet here this

morning and I'm all fagged out from sweeping and cleaning the yard, shaking blankets, cooking, fetching water, bathing children, and there's still the floor inside to sweep, and dishes to wash and myself to bathe — it's endless!

Or again:

Have you an extra onion to give me until tomorrow? If so, I'd appreciate it. I'm trying to do something with these awful beans and I've run out of all my seasonings and spices. A neighbour brought us some spinach last night so we're in the green. I've got dirty clothes galore to wash and iron today.

Or:

I'm sending the kids over to get 10 minutes' peace in which to restore my equilibrium. It looks as if rain is threatening. Please send them back immediately so they won't get caught out in it. Any fiction at your house? I could use some light diversion.

And, very typical . . .

This has been a very hectic morning! First I was rushing to finish a few letters to send to you to post for me. Then it began to sprinkle slightly and I remembered you have no raincoat, so I decided to dash over there myself with the letters and the post key. At the very moment I was stepping out of the door, in stepped someone and that solved the letter posting problem, but I still don't know whether there is any mail for me. I've lost my p.o. box key! Did the children perhaps drop it out of that purse when they were playing with it at your house yesterday?

Or my son keeps getting every kind of chest ailment and I prefer to decide it's the worst:

What's this about whooping cough! Who diagnosed it? Didn't you say he had all his shots and vaccinations? The D.P.T. doesn't require a booster until after he's five years old. Diphtheria-Pertussis (Whooping cough) — Tetanus is one of the most reliable vaccinations I know all three of mine and I have had hoarse, dry coughs but certainly it wasn't whooping cough. Here's Dr Spock to reassure you!

Sometimes, too, conversations get all tangled up and the African night creeps all about and the candles are not lit and

58

the conversation gets more entangled, intense; and the children fall asleep on the floor dazed by it all. The next day I get a book flung at me with vigorous exasperation! 'Here's C.P. Snow. Read him, dammit! And dispel a bit of that fog in thy cranium.'

I am dazed, too, by Mr C.P. Snow. Where do I begin to understand the industrial use of electronics, atomic energy, automation in a world of mud-huts? What is a machine tool? he asks. What are the Two Cultures and the Scientific Revolution? The argument could be quaint to one who hasn't even one leg of culture to stand on. But it isn't really, because even a bush village in Africa begins to feel the tug and pull of the spider-web of life. Would Mr Snow or someone please write me an explanation of what a machine tool is? I'd like to know. My address is. Serowe, Bechuanaland, Africa.

The trouble with the woman from America is that people would rather hold off, sensing her world to be shockingly apart from theirs. But she is a new kind of American or even maybe will be a new kind of African. There isn't anyone here who does not admire her — to come from a world of chicken, hamburgers, TV, escalators and what not to a village mud-hut and a life so tough, where the most you can afford to eat is ground millet and boiled meat. Sometimes you cannot afford to eat at all. Always you have to trudge miles for a bucket of water and carry it home on your head. And to do all this with loud, ringing, sprawling laughter!

Black people in America care much about Africa and she has come here on her own as an expression of that love and concern. Through her, too, one is filled with wonder for a country that breeds individuals about whom, without and within, rushes the wind of freedom. I have to make myself clear, though. She is a different person who has taken by force what America will not give black people. We had some here a while ago, sent out by the State Department. They were very jolly and sociable, but for the most innocent questions they kept saying: 'We can't talk about the government. That's politics. We can't talk politics.' Why did they come here if they were so afraid of what the American government thinks about what they might think or say in

Africa? Why were they so afraid? Africa is not alive for them. It seems a waste of the State Department's money. It seems so strange a thing to send people on goodwill projects if they are so afraid that they jump at the slightest shadow. Why are they so afraid of the government of America which is a government of freedom and democracy? Here we are all afraid of authority and we never pretend anything else. Black people who are sent here by the State Department are tied up in some deep and shameful hypocrisy. It is a terrible pity because such things are destructive to them and hurtful to us.

The woman from America loves both Africa and America, independently. She can take what she wants from us both and say: 'Dammit!' It is a difficult thing to do.

Chief Sekoto holds Court

Even those who did not like chiefs had to concede that Paramount Chief Sekoto was a very charming man. His charm lay not so much in his outer appearance as in his very cheerful outlook on life. In fact, so fond was he of the sunny side of life that he was inclined to regard any gloomy, pessimistic person as insane and make every effort to avoid his company. It was his belief that a witty answer turneth away wrath and that the oil of reason should always be poured on troubled waters.

Every weekday morning, Chief Sekoto listened to cases brought before his court, while the afternoons were spent at leisure unless there were people who had made appointments to interview him. This particular Monday morning a lively and rowdy case was in session when, out of the corner of his eye, Chief Sekoto saw his brother Matenge drive up and park his car opposite the open clearing where court was held. Nothing upset Chief Sekoto more than a visit from his brother, whom he had long classified as belonging to the insane part of mankind. He determined to dally over the proceedings for as long as possible in the hope that his brother would become bored and leave. Therefore he turned his full attention on the case at hand.

The case had been brought in from one of the outlying villages, called Bodibeng, and the cause of its rowdiness was that the whole village of Bodibeng had turned up to witness the trial. A certain old woman of the village, named Mma-Baloi, was charged with allegedly practising witchcraft, and so certain were the villagers of her guilt that they frequently forgot themselves and burst out into loud chatter and had to be brought to order by the president of the court with threats of fines.

Evidence was that Mma-Baloi had always lived a secret and mysterious life apart from the other villagers. She was also in the habit of receiving strangers from far-off places into her home who would not state what dealings they had with Mma-Baloi. Now, over a certain period, a number of the children of the village had died sudden deaths, and each time a mother stood up to describe these sudden deaths, the crowd roared in fury because the deaths of the children and the evil practices of Mma-Baloi were one and the same thing in their minds. The accused, Mma-Baloi, sat a little apart from the villagers in a quaking, ashen, crumpled heap and each time the villagers roared, she seemed about to sink into the earth. Noting this, Chief Sekoto's kindly heart was struck with pity.

Further evidence was that about a week ago a strange young woman had turned up in the village of Bodibeng and made straight for the hut of Mma-Baloi, where she had died a sudden death. This had made Mma-Baloi run screaming from her hut, and it was only the intervention of the police that had saved Mma-Baloi from being torn to pieces by the villagers.

Chief Sekoto was silent for some time. The insanity of mankind never ceased to amaze him. At last he turned to the accused and said gently, 'Well, mother, what do you have to say in defence of yourself?'

'Sir, I am no witch', said the quavering old voice. 'Even though I am called the mother of the witches, I am no witch. Long ago I was taught by the people who live in the bush how to cure ailments with herbs and that is my business.'

She pointed a shaking finger at a bag placed near her.

'I would like to see the contents of the bag', Chief Sekoto said with a great show of interest. The bag was brought to him and its contents tipped out on the ground. They were a various assortment of dried leaves, roots, and berries. He examined them leisurely, picking up a few items for closer inspection. This very deliberate gesture was meant to puncture a hole in the confidence of the crowd, who annoyed him. While he fiddled about he was aware of how silent and intent they had become, following his every movement with their eyes. Thus holding the stage, he turned to the old woman and said:

'Proceed with your defence, mother.'

'About the deaths of the children of which I am accused, I

know nothing, sir', she said. 'About the young woman who died in my home last Saturday, I am also innocent. This young woman came to me on recommendation, being grievously ill. We were discussing the ailment when she fell dead at my feet. Never has such a thing occurred before, and this caused me to lose my mind and run out of the house.'

'That is quite understandable, mother', Chief Sekoto said sympathetically. 'Even I should have been grieved if some stranger was struck with death in my home.'

He swept the crowd with a stern glance. 'Who issues the certificates of death in Bodibeng?' he asked.

There was a short, bewildered silence. Then a car and a messenger had to be found to fetch the doctor of the Bodibeng hospital. There was a delay of two hours as the doctor was engaged in an operation. Throughout this long wait the court remained in session. At one stage Chief Sekoto received an impatient note: 'Dear Brother', it said. 'Please spare a few moments to discuss an urgent matter.'

Chief Sekoto replied: 'Is it life or death? I am at the moment faced with the life or death of an old woman. I cannot move.'

It was near noon when the doctor arrived. His evidence was brief and to the point. Yes, it was true, he said. There had been a surprising number of child deaths in the village of Bodibeng, and death in each case had been due to pneumonia; and yes, he said, he had performed a postmortem on the body of a young woman last Saturday afternoon. The young woman had died of a septic womb due to having procured an abortion with a hooked and unsterilised instrument. He would say that the septic condition of the womb had been of three months' duration.

All that was left now was for Chief Sekoto to pass judgement on the case. This he did sternly, drawing himself up to his full height.

'People of Bodibeng', he said. 'It seems to me you are all suffering from derangement of the brain.'

He paused long enough to allow the villagers to look at each other uneasily.

'Your children die of pneumonia', he thundered, 'and to

63

shield yourselves from blame you accuse a poor old woman of having bewitched them into death. Not only that. You falsely accuse her of a most serious crime which carries the death sentence. How long have you planned the death of a poor old woman, deranged people of Bodibeng? How long have you caused her to live in utter misery, suspicion, and fear? I say: Can dogs bark for ever? Oh no, people of Bodibeng, today you will make payment for the legs of the old mother who has fled before your barking. I say: The fault is all with you, and because of this I fine each household of Bodibeng one beast. From the money that arises out of the sale of these beasts, each household is to purchase warm clothing for the children so that they may no longer die of pneumonia.'

He turned and looked at the old woman, changing his expression to one of kindness.

'As for you, mother', he said. 'I cannot allow you to go and live once more among the people of Bodibeng. It is only hatred that the people of Bodibeng feel for you, and this has driven them out of their minds. As hatred never dies, who knows what evil they will not plot against you. I have a large house, and you are welcome to the protection it offers. Besides, I suffer from an ailment for which I am always given penicillin injections at the hospital. Now I am tired of the penicillin injections and perhaps your good herbs may serve to cure me of my troubles.'

He stood up, signifying the end of the case. The people of Bodibeng fled in confusion from the courtyard, but the old woman sat for a long time on the ground, silent tears of gratitude dripping down into her lap.

Property

He had paid for his wife with twelve head of cattle and the marriage had been arranged by an uncle, one of the elder brothers of his mother. She should therefore have been his property, an impersonal something acquired to assist his mother in tilling the fields, fetching water from the river, collecting firewood from the bush and cooking the meals. But there was something wrong somehow and after the first few weeks of marriage the young wife sensed it and it unnerved her.

True enough, she was well-trained in the duties of a wife and of an apparently docile subservient temperament as women of her background are supposed to be; but in reality she was as lovely as the tall cool grasses that swayed in the summer wind. At least, the man saw her that way with his own magic eyes. People were all kinds of things to him: nothing like the dull pretentious clothes of custom which they all wore; but in flashes, and at moments of crisis they revealed their real selves: some were giant icy mountains, some were wide wind-swept plains in breadth of thought and depth of suffering; some were stark bare twigs perpetually bent before the storms and winters of life and some, like his mother were the evening sunsets. And because his wife was young she had no way of concealing that she was the grass that swayed in the summer wind. This caused him to look at her with a strange delight in his eyes and a quiet half-smile about his mouth. She always dropped her eyes in embarrassment because she could not understand it.

'Perhaps I have married a mad man', she thought with fear in her heart, longing for the thoughtless, chattering companionship of her sisters.

And she became more and more sure of this as the days passed. One evening when they were alone in their hut, the man enquired gently:

'Are you tired?'

She looked at him in a quick suspicious way and bent her head with an equally quick movement for that smile about his mouth and that awful look was in his eyes as though he was silently pleading for more than the contract allowed. No slave owner asked a purchased slave if the slave was tired. In fact, if something was your property you expected it to keep the place spick and span and occasionally you roughed it up with a good beating to keep it in its place; to assert your male dominance. But these beatings were profitable to the purchased slave's family. The slave ran home and the condition of return was that its family be made richer by one beast. The young wife wondered how she would ever be able to provoke the necessary quarrel with this soft, unmanly man. Yet there was nothing unmanly about his love-making at night and this one direct, though inarticulate, expression of his love she confused, to her regret, with the mistaken feeling that he was the slave of her body.

A change took place. It was the young wife who began to dominate the household because she despised her husband and hated her mother-in-law whom she privately blamed for the womanliness of her husband and it seemed to her as though there was a conspiracy of secret understanding between them. They looked so alike. They smiled alike and had a way of communicating with each other by a mere glance. And really, contrary to custom, the man had grown up almost entirely under the influence of his mother. The men of the family clan, who should have accepted responsibility for him after his father had died when he was barely one year old, turned out to be a restless lot with their hearts drawn to the big cities of South Africa. But they were always sending money home for the purchase of cattle and then always in one way or another getting killed in the cities. Thus, the man eventually found himself almost the sole inheritor of huge herds of cattle. On the other hand, the young wife's family had clung to the old tribal way of life. They were a large clan with few beasts and their joy and greed and relief were great at the marriage of one of their own to the richest man in the area.

A little of this clan greed made the young wife careless of

her behaviour. A flounce developed in her walk and a contemptuous smile often played around her mouth. The mother was quick to notice these things and though she often looked at her son anxiously, she said nothing. The son, meanwhile, was still wrapped in his own vision of a woman who walked like grass that swayed in the summer wind.

But very soon a certain incident brought him out of the clouds. One evening he noticed that his wife had a deep cut on her arm and in his odd gentle fashion enquired the cause, whereupon she burst into laughter. He could not mistake the contempt in her eyes and without a word, he stood up and left the room, not to appear again that night, nor three nights after that. On the fourth day the young wife was goaded through frustration into remarking that the man sought comfort from his mother; whereupon the man picked up a thick stick and beat her severely; whereupon the young wife ran home. The family were overjoyed. The bruises and bumps were immense. They would demand three head of cattle as compensation.

Days passed and no word arrived demanding the return of the young wife. The family's joy turned to anxiety and an elder of the clan was sent to enquire the cause.

'Tell them that I no longer require her as my wife', the man said.

Anxiety turned to alarm but the man seemed stone deaf and blind to any appeal. Cunning persuasion was turned on the mother. The young wife was expecting a child. Who knows, it might be a boy to carry on the family name. And so, in turn, the mother persuaded the son to accept his wife back. In relief, the young wife's family forgot to press for the compensation of the three beasts.

Back in her routine, the young wife found that things had indeed changed. That magic look and half-smile had disappeared from her husband's face and you could not tell him apart from all the other men of the area. Theirs was a normal marriage at last.

But it was barely a month later that the man left the reserve for the city and barely a month passed before the two women received the news that he had been killed in the city.

The two women did not grieve long, however, for six months later a son was born in the exact image of his father. They called him Mbuya, which means, he-has-come-back. And this event drew the two women close together. The child was their whole life and he grew up in an excess of womanly smothering and petting. As he was to inherit such huge herds of cattle, neither woman gave a thought to his education. The boy Mbuya remedied this omission in an unexpected way on the day he turned fourteen years old.

His birthday was also kept as a family feast day for his dead father and early that morning his mother asked him to take a goat to her old home where the feast was held. On delivering the goat, his maternal grandmother ordered two of his cousins to prepare him some tea. These cousins had been to the city for an education and were in the process of training to be teachers. They were snobbish about it and as soon as the grandmother was out of earshot one of the cousins passed a remark that so wounded the boy that he almost fainted on the spot.

'Hmm', she said. 'I really don't know why the old hag orders us to make tea for such an uneducated person. He ought to be our servant. I suppose we must honour him for his wealth.'

He cried silently: 'Stop, you are hurting me.'

But they chattered on in their artificial manner.

'Really', said the other. 'We must get back to civilisation as soon as possible.'

And they both turned and gave the boy a nasty look to emphasise what they thought about making tea for uneducated people.

At the first opportunity, the boy mentioned his new plans to his mother.

'I am going to school', he said.

She opened her eyes in surprise.

'Why?' she asked. 'One day you will be the richest man in the district and where have you ever heard of a rich man who needs an education? Education is for those who have to work.'

'Is that so?' he said. 'Well then, I shall slaughter all the cattle.'

His mother had had some frightening experiences with the stubborn, wilful spirit in him. In distress she fled to the paternal grandmother. The paternal grandmother bent her eyes to hide their gleam of joy: 'The spirit of my son is indeed in the boy', she thought.

Aloud she said: 'You must take the boy to the city for his education.'

Her family clan objected strenuously. They thought of the boy and the cattle as their possession and they feared what an education might do to him. He above all had to stay in the old way of life, till by some natural gravitational law this huge wealth fell into their hands, oh, maybe when the paternal grandmother died. And all the while the boy secretly threatened the mother with the slaughter of the cattle. She knew he would do it. There was something in him which was capable of anything.

The day they left for the city he made a silent vow: 'I shall never return.'

He started at the bottom and by the time he was twenty-six he had completed matriculation. What next? And while he stopped to think, certain happenings in the city attracted his attention. One of these is politics and since he concentrated on politics as much as he had on his studies, he was soon jailed for two years. On release from jail he was considered an African who was unfit to live in the city and given a restriction order to remain permanently in his tribal reserve.

The day of his arrival back home, the young man Mbuya, noticed a vast crowd of maternal aunts, uncles and so on assembling in the yard of his paternal grandmother's home. Soon his mother said:

'Pay attention, my son.'

Then one of the elders of the clan spoke:

'I wish to enquire, on behalf of the family, if there is anything wrong with you, my son.'

The young man looked them over warily. He was not sure what they wanted and he had a need to escape in a few days.

'There is nothing wrong with me, uncle', he said.

'We are very pleased to hear that, my son', the elder said.

'Now, since you are in good health, we further wish to enquire as to why you have not married.'

'I have not had the time', he said, surprised, yet on guard.

'That is what we thought too, my son', continued the elder. 'Accordingly, we have arranged for a suitable marriage partner for you. The general agreement was that if you do not marry we shall lose you.'

The young man kept silent awhile. Then he said:

'I hope someone will agree to abide with this poor girl because I cannot.'

'Please explain', said the elder.

'I have a different view of my future wife', he said. 'For one thing, I shall choose her for myself. For another, my wife shall never be property. She will never be purchased to be the slave in my mother's home. She will never carry a pot of water on her head and she will never collect firewood in the bush. As for the cattle which belong to me, you may all do with them as you wish.'

There was a brief, stunned silence. The women started a terrible wail. His eyes passed casually over the gathering. He did not care. He really did not care and he felt so detached as though no one had ever belonged to him. What startled him, however, was the expression on the face of his paternal grandmother. Even when addressed by the elder, she could not suppress the fact that she had been smiling:

'Tell us, Elder Sister, about the mentality of this child', said the elder.

'He has this tendency to know his own mind', she said. 'Younger sister and I have often been amazed to note that he is one person whose word and deed agree. Due to this we avoided any interference in the child's life. I am most anxious that you therefore do nothing rash about this proposed marriage as we shall indeed create a problem for the maiden.'

And the young man was not aware of his rudeness. He had an escape plan to work out. The discussion seemed un-ending. He stood up abruptly and looked at the gathering; absent-mindedly, distantly. He even smiled, perhaps seeing in his mind's eye a magic life they would never know. Only his mother recognised it, that magic look and half-smile that had so terrified her when she was a woman who walked like the grass swaying in the summer wind.

A Power Struggle

The universe had a more beautiful dream. It was not the law of the jungle or the survival of the fittest but a dream that had often been the priority of saints — the power to make evil irrelevant. All the people of Southern Africa had lived out this dream before the dawn of the colonial era. Time and again it shed its beam of light on their affairs although the same patterns of horror would arise like dark engulfing waves.

It was as though once people had lived in settled communities for any length of time, hostilities of an intolerable nature developed due to power struggles, rivalries and jealousies. Not all the stories were attractive or coherent; they were often so direct and brutal that it was almost like darkness destroying darkness and no rule was untainted by it. It was before these fierce passions for power that people often gave way and it formed the base of the tangled story of tribal movement and migration. When it was all over only a tree, a river bank, a hill or a mountain lingered in the memory as the dwelling place of a tribe.

There were two brothers of the Tlabina clan, Davhana and Baeli. In more ways than one Davhana was destined to rule. He was the born heir to the throne and in acknowledgement of this, the old chief, their father, had, once his health began to fail him, handed to Davhana the sacred rain-making apparatus — a symbol of his destiny. But Davhana was also a fearfully rich personality with glowing black eyes. There was about him the restless beauty of the earth in motion and he could laugh for so long and so loudly that his laughter was like the sound of the wind rushing across the open plains. He was tall and strongly-built with lithe, agile movements. People humorously accorded to him the formal and often meaningless titles a king held as his due such as 'Beautiful One' or 'Great Lion' but unlike other kings, Davhana earned them with his living personality. In spite of this his succession was not assured and his destiny took an unpredictable turn.

They were at the burial ceremony for their father when his brother, Baeli, abruptly threw down the first challenge to his succession. It was Davhana's right as his father's successor to turn the first sod in his grave. It was also a confirmation before the assembled people that he would rule. Davhana had his digging implement raised but his younger brother, Baeli, stepped in ahead of him and turned the first sod. The older brother stepped back instantly, his digging implement relaxed at his side. He flung his head back with an impatient gesture and stared at the horizon, his mouth curled down in contempt. The younger brother straightened up quietly. He too looked into the distance, a smile on his lips and menace in his eyes. The gestures were so unexpected that the assembled people stirred instinctively and stifled gasps of surprise swept through the crowd. There was not anyone present who did not know that the succession was open to dispute.

Immediately, the dispute did not concern the people. The real power struggle would take place in the inner circle of relatives and councillors. It was often an impersonal process as far as the mass of the people were concerned — what they respected was not so much a chief in person as the position he occupied. And yet, there seemed a contradiction in this. It was real men of passion who fought for that position and should an evil man gain the throne, people would suffer. People had a number of cynical attitudes to cover such events. One of their attitudes was: 'We pay homage to all the chief's sons, since which one of them will finally become chief is uncertain . . .' If things became too disruptive a large number of men would suddenly remember that they had not branded their cattle or attended to their everyday affairs.

The two young men of passion turned away from the funeral ceremony and walked side by side for some distance; Davhana purposefully keeping pace with his brother.

'Baeli', he asked in his direct way. 'Why did you turn the first sod on father's grave? It was my duty by right! You have shamed me in front of all the people! Why did you do it?'

He listened with his whole body for his brother's reply but no reply was forthcoming — only the pacing of their feet walking in unison filled the silence. Davhana looked sideways at his brother's face. Baeli stared straight ahead; the smile still lingered around his mouth and there was an aloofness in his eyes. Had they in such an abrupt manner suddenly recognised that they were total strangers to each other? A day ago they had shared a youth together, hunted together and appeared to laugh at the same jokes. Only Davhana felt the pain. His personality radiated outwards, always reaching towards love and friendship. His brother's personality turned inwards into a whirlpool of darkness. He felt himself being dragged down into that whirlpool and instinctively he turned and walked off in his own direction.

Davhana walked until he reached a clearing outside the village. Evening was approaching. The night was warm. A full yellow moon arose behind a small hill in the distance. The atmosphere was deeply silent and still. The subdued murmurs of insects in the grass were peaceful and sweet. The young man settled himself on the earth and was soon lost in his own thoughts. Now and then he sighed deeply as though he were reaching a crossroad with himself, as though he were drawing to himself the scattered fragments of his youthful life. He had lived with the reckless generosity of his personality and nothing in his past seemed a high peak. He had lived, danced, eaten and sung in the full enjoyment of the pleasures of the moment. The events of the day cast their dark shadows over him.

Softly approaching footsteps stirred him out of his reverie. The moonlight outlined the form of one of the elders of the tribe. Davhana turned his head with his glowing look, inviting the old man to seat himself. The old man squatted low beside his reclining form and stared for some time in a detached way at the small hill behind which the moon had arisen.

'Do your thoughts trouble you, Beautiful One?' the old man asked at last. 'I have stood here for some time and heard you sigh and sigh.'

'Oh no, Uncle', the young man said, with a vigorous shake of his head. 'Nothing troubles me. If I sigh it may be only for a carefree youth which I am about to lose.'

The elder plucked at a few strands of grass and continued to stare at the distant hill.

'Everyone took note today of the awful deed your brother committed', he said. 'It was the most awful breach of good manners and some of us are questioning its motive.'

The young man curled his mouth in contempt again as though it were beneath him to recognise avarice and ambition.

'Baeli has always had strange tendencies', he said. 'Though I have liked him as my brother.'

The old man kept silent a while. When he spoke his voice was as sweet and peaceful as the subdued murmurs of the insects in the grass.

'I have come to teach you a few things about life', he said. 'People have never been given a gift like you before, Beautiful One, and they look eagerly forward to your rule because they think that a time of prosperity and happiness lies before them. All these years you have lived with the people and your ways were good to them. When a man built his yard you stopped to tie a knot in the rafters and the hunting spoils you shared generously with all your men, never demanding an abundant share for yourself. You spread happiness and laughter wherever you travelled. People understand these qualities. They are the natural gifts of a good man. But these very gifts can be a calamity in a ruler. A ruler has to examine the dark side of human life and understand that men belong to that darkness. There are many men born with inadequate gifts and this disturbs them. They have no peace within themselves and once their jealousy is aroused they do terrible things . . .'

The old man hesitated, uncertain of how to communicate his alarms and fears. A ruler could only reach the day of installation without bloodshed provided no other member of his family had declared his ambition publicly. Baeli had publicly declared his ambition and it needed only a little of that poison for all sorts of perverse things to happen. They had some horrible things in their history. They had been ruled by all sorts of lunatics and mental defectives who had mutually poisoned or assassinated each other. His grandfather had been poisoned by a brother who had in turn been assassinated by another brother. Not even Davhana's father's rule was untainted by it — there were several assassinations behind his father's peaceful and lengthy reign.

You will soon find out the rules of life, Beautiful One', the old man murmured. 'You will have to kill or be killed.'

The young man said nothing in reply. The old man sat bathed in moonlight and the subdued murmurs of insects in the grass were peaceful and sweet.

The struggle that unfolded between Davhana and his brother was so subtle that it was difficult to deal with. It took place when men sat deep in council debating the issues of the day. There was always a point at which Baeli could command all the attention to himself and in doing so make his brother, Davhana, irrelevant. Baeli would catch a debate just at the point at which his brother had spoken and while a question or statement trembled in the air awaiting a reply, Baeli would step in and deflect men's thoughts in a completely new direction, thus making the previous point completely invalid. Some men began to enjoy this game and daily, Davhana rapidly lost ground with them. He refused at crucial points to assert his power and allowed dialogues to drift away from him. He indulged in no counter-intrigue when it became evident from the laughter of the men that his brother had begun to intrigue with them.

When they moved into the dark side of the moon, the most fearful massacre took place. Davhana alone escaped with his life and fled into the dark night. He had a wound in his right shoulder where a spear had pierced him as he lay asleep in his hut. He did not know who had stabbed him but in the confusion of the struggle in the dark he broke free of the hands that lunged at him and escaped.

Once, during his flight in the dark, Davhana paused again and took stock of his destiny. It was still scattered and fragmentary but the freshness and beauty of his youth lay on him like a protective mantle. If power was the unfocused demoniacal stare of his brother then he would have none of that world. Nothing had paralysed, frustrated and enraged him more than that stare.

'He can take all that he desires', Davhana thought. 'I shall not go back there. I want to live.'

He chose for himself that night the life of one who would

take refuge where he could find it and so he continued his flight into the night.

The people of the Tlabina clan awoke the following morning to a new order. They had a murderer as their ruler. Baeli had slain whatever opposition he was likely to encounter and no one was immediately inclined to oppose him. The ritual of installation proceeded along its formal course. When Baeli appeared a chorus of adulation greeted him and everyone present made humble obeisance. The usual speeches were made to the impersonal office of kingship.

After three moons had waxed and waned word travelled back to the people that their ruler, Davhana, was alive and well and had sought refuge with a powerful Pedi clan. The people of the Tlabina clan began to vanish from their true home, sometimes in large groupings, sometimes in small trickles until they had abandoned Baeli. If the wild dogs ate him, who knows?

A power struggle was the great dialogue of those times and many aspects of the dialogue were touched by the grandeur of kings like Davhana. It was hardly impersonal as living men always set the dialogue in motion. They forced people under duress to make elaborate choices between good and evil. This thread of strange philosophical beauty was deeply woven into the history of the land and the story was repeated many times over so that it became the only history people ever knew.

With the dawn of the colonial era this history was subdued. A new order was imposed on life. People's kings rapidly faded from memory and became myths of the past. No choices were left between what was good and what was evil. There was only slavery and exploitation.

A Period of Darkness

The small hill was a few hundred yards away from the village. A few tall trees dotted the hillside. In the early morning summer light the birds in the trees continued their mating and preparation of their homes for their young ones. There was a constant rustle of activity as they mated lightly and dizzily on thin strips of branches, fluffed out their feathers or spun in somersaults as they wove nests out of long strands of fresh grass. Now and then they took time off from their labours and rested wide-eyed and absent-minded on the branches. Or suddenly, they would sing. They were un-disturbed by the presence of a silent man seated beneath one of the tall trees. He was somewhat like them, a family man who had mated and prepared his home for his young ones.

A long night of brooding reflection had passed for the silent man. He was disturbed by the pain of one who had been dispossessed and for many hours he sat and looked down at the land and the huts, its life towards him. He was an outcast, alone with his pain. Eventually, uncertainly, unsteadily, he arose to his feet and from the bark of the trees, he made a long twine.

It was until the year 1823 that Chief Motswasele II, ruled the people of Bakwena tribe and all through his rule, which lasted a number of years, people fell into a period of darkness. Although people were always prepared to make obeisance to an hereditary ruler, the tradition of rulership and its relation-ship to the people was a sacred one. It was regarded that a ruler only existed because there were people to rule. He could not rule by himself and had to put all matters of government before the people; without a public discussion of every event, there was no rule. And so a vast mosaic of government had been built up with its origins lost in time and which made the whole society a permanent dialogue and debate. But the relationship of the ruled to the ruler went deeper than that. It was that of a father governing a vast family with many

78

problems, so that in reality a chief had to be born with a heart which bleeds or invent one along the way as every human problem and difficulty was placed before him.

Chief Motswasele reversed this order. During his rule people ceased to exist and his demented activities gained precedence over everything else. He took other men's wives for himself and also allowed his court favourites to do the same, without fear of punishment or penalty. He helped himself freely to the cattle and other property of his people and due to his aberrant activities he often imposed the death penalty on people.

It was as though in his early rule he paid lip service to all the courtesies demanded by tradition, because a period of suffering ensued before people realised that they were hopelessly degraded. He was the sort of ruler people had rarely encountered and initially a phenomenon almost impossible to deal with.

He was so impossible to deal with partly because in tradition people regarded themselves as the property of the chief and partly the unspeakable had crept up on them unawares. Nearly all chiefs were slightly tainted with the evils of Motswasele but they committed these evils very covertly and secretly. Motswasele committed all his evils quite openly. Over the years he had become loathsome to people and, in keeping with his way of life, he wore a permanent sneer on his face. Protests against him were only made in soft whispers around the village.

It was a demented village of hysteria and fright. For a long while people had presented each other with a wide range of laughter and hysteria in order that they might live with the unspeakable. They had learned to close their eyes and ears to many things: who had been murdered? Whose property appropriated? Whose home defiled? They did not know because an incautious look or an incautious word had often resulted in the death penalty.

It appeared initially as if the deaths of the man, Leungo, and his wife, Keeme, would pass into the stream of general horrors they lived with. The story followed a stream of the same pattern; soft whispers of the point at which Leungo's wife had been accosted by the Chief. They knew he was away from home with a party of other men on a hunting expedition.

They knew of the agitated efforts his family had made to send a messenger to him to ward him off from home. They knew how the secret messenger had in turn been accosted and threatened so that there was no one to warn the man that his home had been invaded. They knew how he had come home late that night and parted silently from his hunting companions. They knew how his wife had heard his footsteps and how that frightened and tremulous cry had rent the silence of the night: 'You cannot come in! The Chief is here!'

They knew how he had halted cautiously, one foot raised and equally cautiously retreated from his home. Up until that point many men knew the story quite well. They knew that the Chief experienced an immense pleasure at that point, like an ailing person. A woman was only desirable to him if she was the possession of another man. At that point many men had disappeared from the village. There were many other villages, not too far distant and they disappeared there and faded their lives into a quiet oblivion.

The man, Leungo, did not retreat far — only a few hundred yards away from the village. On awakening that morning, the whole village knew of the silent man on the hill. After a few quick surprised looks everyone turned away and minded their own affairs. The joke belonged to the Chief and his favourites. What was the man trying to do? Was he making a challenge?

It was one of the little herdboys who shattered the nervous system of the village. Towards evening of that day he had absent-mindedly driven his flock of goats past the small hill with its few tall trees, looked up and seen the man, Leungo, hanging there. Suicide was an almost unknown form of death in those days and the sight of the dead man, so solitary and alone, had almost driven the little boy out of his mind. At first he walked through the village weeping loudly. When people caught hold of him and tried to quieten him down, his hysteria was frenzied. It took hours to calm him.

Then tragedy was added to tragedy. It was reported in the

village that the wife of Leungo had also hanged herself. Then what remained of his family simply disappeared during the night; no one knew whence. In the morning no sign remained of the tragedy: all the bodies had been silently removed. Only the empty homestead and animals remained to be plundered by the Chief and his favourites.

An angry whisper swept through the village: 'While we were asleep last night the wizard did his daily duty . . .'

From then onwards men's eyes became a hard, blank, uncommunicative stare, a wall behind which everything was shut up, where thoughts and feelings were strictly private and never shared. Yet those hard blank stares could swiftly alternate into looks of friendly casualness and ease. A peculiar kind of dialogue started in the village. No names were mentioned and yet a full dialogue ensued in brief words and gestures. Extraordinary statements of quietude and tenderness were made.

In their haste to remove the body the henchmen of the Chief had forgotten Leungo's hunting bag which lay beneath the tall tree. Someone found it there and secretly brought it back to the village. The men behaved as if they did not possess hunting bags of their own. The contents of Leungo's bag were opened and examined, tenderly. It was filled with the dried meat of animals and wild fruit and berries. For weeks it was passed from man to man and for weeks the quality of Leungo's household was a favoured topic of discussion.

Although people lived their communal dream, each family was renowned for its own ways. Some were renowned for their food and beer; some for their skills in tanning and leather work; some for their rich harvests of crop and some were renowned above all for human qualities. The home of the man, Leungo, and his wife, Keeme, was renowned for its warmth, peace and order. Due to this contentment in the home both husband and wife often had an abstracted look in their eyes. They wanted nothing beyond all they had. People perfectly comprehended why the man had not fled away to another village. He was happy in his home and would rather die than part from it.

They were like stones lying scattered apart and slowly, they all came together. There was no strength in stones when they lay apart. They began to cast eyes around for another ruler, a certain intention being clear in their minds. There were two powerful men in the village, one Segokotlo and the other Moruakgomo. Segokotlo was the younger brother of Motswasele and Moruakgomo was the son of a regent, Tshosa, who had ruled the tribe when Motswasele was as yet too young to rule. Moruakgomo was highly favoured as he had a tall strong physique and a loud ringing voice. Very soon he was included in the night-time plotting and strange dialogue.

'In our custom', the men asked obscurely, 'who is it who eats last?' 'It is the father of the household who eats last', replied Moruakgomo. 'He eats last because he has to see to the well-being of others.' 'A bird with long talons is not good to eat', the men said, softly throwing him another riddle. Interpreted it meant that the people no longer found Motswasele a desirable person to associate with.

And so the obscure dialogue worked itself to the point where it became clear that the people wanted to rid themselves of Motswasele in an unpleasant way. Moruakgomo at first resisted the idea, cutting through the obscurities with a clear statement. 'It is not the custom to kill a Chief', he said. 'The jackal will never change his ways of trotting', they said, indicating that their position and stand were final.

There was no precedent for killing a Chief. If it ever happened then or later it was a most rare occurrence; the society was too moral and balanced. But when the time and place were ready Moruakgomo gave his consent to the secret plan.

In the meanwhile Motswasele was deceived as to the exact mood of the people. The village appeared more relaxed than usual and a mood of casual friendliness and ease pervaded everything. One day he sent out word that the regiments were to prepare themselves for war and gather outside the village on an appointed day. The men responded with vigour. All were prepared to assemble outside the village with their weapons and wait instructions for war.

War was also one of the grievances they held against Motswasele. Over the period of his twenty year rule, he had involved the tribe in dishonour. He had sent the regiments into war against such tribes as the Kgalagadi who were poor and owned no cattle. He had sent them into battle against tribes weaker than they and kept the area in a state of constant strife and disruption.

Eagerly therefore did the men assemble on the appointed day in the open space outside the village. With patient expressions they listened as Motswasele addressed them about the nature of the present war. Then it was the turn of Moruakgomo to arise and recite a praise poem, stirring the men to battle in his loud, ringing voice. Loud and clear his voice was but something was wrong with the praise poem. It was not one of praise. It was one of condemnation. It began . . .

'A Chief when fashioned must be fine, fashioned with proper hands . . .'

The poem then went on ominously listing all the evils of Motswasele, the wars of dishonour, the defilement of men's homes, the wanton robbery of their cattle and property. It was so unexpected that it took Motswasele some time to recognise his predicament. Then he slowly raised his head. His eyes widened with fear as he looked out at the assembled men. He opened his mouth, silently gasping for breath. And so he died, with wide-open, terror-stricken eyes. For the men arose and, instead of moving off to war, they moved towards him and one by one cast their spears into his body.

When the deed was done, they seated themselves near the assassination area, opened their snuff-horns and treated each other to snuff. They took time off from their labours and rested wide-eyed and absent-minded. It was but a brief pause because in those days people's history progressed with strife and bloodshed. The tribe was soon to be dispersed to the four corners of the earth in the battle that took place between Moruakgomo and Segokotlo for succession to the Chieftainship.

But in that brief pause a triumphant statement was made — that people had always held a position of ascendency in matters of government, that people had always lived with the glimmerings of a true democracy.

The Lovers

The love affair began in the summer. The love affair began in those dim dark days when young men and women did not have love affairs. It was one of those summers when it rained in torrents. Almost every afternoon towards sunset the low-hanging, rain-filled clouds would sweep across the sky in packed masses and suddenly, with barely a warning, the rain would pour down in blinding sheets.

The young women and little girls were still out in the forest gathering wood that afternoon when the first warning signs of rain appeared in the sky. They hastily gathered up their bundles of wood and began running home to escape the approaching storm. Suddenly, one of the young women halted painfully. In her haste she had trodden on a large thorn.

'Hurry on home, Monosi!' she cried to a little girl panting behind her. 'I have to get this thorn out of my foot. If the rain catches me I shall find some shelter and come home once it is over.'

Without a backward glance the little girl sped on after the hard-running group of wood gatherers. The young woman was quite alone with the approaching storm. The thorn proved difficult to extract. It had broken off and embedded itself deeply in her heel. A few drops of rain beat down on her back. The sky darkened.

Anxiously she looked around for the nearest shelter and saw a cave in some rocks at the base of a hill nearby. She picked up her bundle of wood and limped hastily towards it, with the drops of rain pounding down faster and faster. She had barely entered the cave when the torrent unleashed itself in a violent downpour. Her immediate concern was to seek sanctuary but a moment later her heart lurched in fear as she realised that she was not alone. The warmth of another human filled the interior. She swung around swiftly and found herself almost face to face with a young man.

'We can shelter here together from the storm', he said

with quiet authority.

His face was as kind and protective as his words. Reassured, the young woman set down her bundle of sticks in the roomy interior of the cave and together they seated themselves near its entrance. The roar of the rain was deafening so that even the thunder was muffled by its intensity. With quiet, harmonious movements the young man undid a leather pouch tied to his waist. He spent all his time cattle-herding and to while away the long hours he busied himself with all kinds of leather work, assembling skins into all kinds of clothes and blankets. He had a large number of sharpened implements in his pouch. He indicated to the young woman that he wished to extract the thorn. She extended her foot towards him and for some time he busied himself with this task, gently whittling away the skin around the thorn until he had exposed it sufficiently enough to extract it.

The young woman looked at his face with interest and marvelled at the ease and comfort she felt in his presence. In their world men and women lived strictly apart, especially the young and unmarried. This sense of apartness and separateness continued even throughout married life and marriage itself seemed to have no significance beyond a union for the production of children. This wide gap between the sexes created embarrassment on the level of personal contact; the young men often slid their eyes away uneasily or giggled at the sight of a woman. The young man did none of this. He had stared her directly in the eyes, all his movements were natural and unaffected. He was also very pleasing to look at. She thanked him with a smile once he had extracted the thorn and folded her extended foot beneath her. The violence of the storm abated a little but the heavily-laden sky continued to pour forth a steady downpour.

She had seen the young man around the village; she could vaguely place his family connections.

'Aren't you the son of Ra-Keaja?' she asked. She had a light chatty voice with an undertone of laughter in it, very expressive of her personality. She liked, above all, to be happy.

'I am the very Keaja he is named after', the young man replied with a smile. 'I am the first-born in the family.'

'I am the first-born in the family, too', she said. 'I am Tselane, the daughter of Mma-Tselane.'

His family ramifications were more complicated than hers. His father had three wives. All the first born of the first, second and third houses were boys. There were altogether eight children, three boys and five girls, he explained. It was only when the conversation became more serious that Tselane realised that a whole area of the young man's speech had eluded her. He was the extreme opposite of the light chatty young woman. He talked from deep rhythms within himself as though he had invented language specifically for his own use. He had an immense range of expression and feeling at his command; now his eyes lit up with humour, then they were absolutely serious and in earnest.

He swayed almost imperceptibly as he talked. He talked like no one she had ever heard talking before, yet all his utterances were direct, simple and forthright. She bent forward and listened more attentively to his peculiar manner of speech.

'I don't like my mother', he said, shocking her. 'I am her only son simply because my father stopped cohabiting with her after I was born. My father and I are alike. We don't like to be controlled by anyone and she made his life a misery when they were newly married. It was as if she had been born with a worm eating at her heart; she is satisfied with nothing. The only way my father could control the situation was to ignore her completely . . .'

He remained silent awhile, concentrating on his own thoughts. 'I don't think I approve of arranged marriages', he said finally. 'My father would never have married her had he had his own choice. He was merely presented with her one day by his family and told that they were to be married and there was nothing he could do about it.'

He kept silent about the torture he endured from his mother. She hated him deeply and bitterly. She had hurled stones at him and scratched him on the arms and legs in her wild frustration. Like his father he eluded her. He rarely spent time at home but kept the cattlepost as his permanent residence. When he approached home it was always with some gift of clothes or blankets. On that particular day he had an enormous gourd filled with milk.

Tselane floundered out of her depth in the face of such stark revelations. They lived the strictest of traditional ways of life, all children were under the control of their parents until they married, therefore it was taboo to discuss their elders. In her impulsive chatty way and partly out of embarrassment, it had been on the tip of her tongue to say that she liked her mother, that her mother was very kind-hearted. But there was a disturbing undertone in her household too. Her mother and father — and she was sure of it due to her detailed knowledge of her mother's way of life — had not cohabited for years either. A few years ago her father had taken another wife. She was her mother's only child. Oh, the surface of their household was polite and harmonious but her father was rarely at home. He was always irritable and morose when he was home.

'I am sorry about all the trouble in your home', she said at last, in a softer, more thoughtful tone. She was shaken at having been abruptly jolted into completely new ways of thought.

The young man smiled and then quite deliberately turned and stared at her. She stared back at him with friendly interest. She did not mind his close scrutiny of her person, he was easy to associate with, comfortable, truthful and open in his every gesture.

'Do you approve of arranged marriages?' he asked, still smiling.

'I have not thought of anything', she replied truthfully.

The dark was approaching rapidly. The rain had trickled down to a fine drizzle. Tselane stood up and picked up her bundle of wood. The young man picked up his gourd of milk. They were barely visible as they walked home together in the dark. Tselane's home was not too far from the hill. She lived on the extreme western side of the village, he on the extreme eastern side.

A bright fire burned in the hut they used as a cooking place on rainy days. Tselane's mother was sitting bent forward on her low stool, listening attentively to a visitor's tale. It was always like this — her mother was permanently surrounded by women who confided in her. The whole story of life unfolded daily around her stool; the ailments of children, women who had just had miscarriages, women undergoing treatment for barren wombs — the story was endless. It was the great pleasure of Tselane to seat herself quietly behind her mother's stool and listen with fascinated ears to this endless tale of woe.

Her mother's visitor that evening was on the tail end of a description of one of her children's ailments; chronic epilepsy, which seemed beyond cure. The child seemed in her death throes and the mother was just at the point of demonstrating the violent seizures when Tselane entered. Tselane quietly set her bundle of wood down in a corner and the conversation continued uninterrupted. She took her favourite place behind her mother's stool. Her father's second wife, Mma-Monosi, was seated on the opposite side of the fire, her face composed and serious. Her child, the little girl Monosi, fed and attended to, lay fast asleep on a sleeping mat in one corner of the hut.

Tselane loved the two women of the household equally. They were both powerful independent women but with sharply differing personalities. Mma-Tselane was a queen who vaguely surveyed the kingdom she ruled, with an abstracted, absent-minded air. Over the years of her married life she had built up a way of life for herself that filled her with content. She was reputed to be very delicate in health as after the birth of Tselane she had suffered a number of miscarriages and seemed incapable of bearing any more children. Her delicate health was a source of extreme irritation to her husband and at some stage he had abandoned her completely and taken Mma-Monosi as his second wife, intending to perpetuate his line and name through her healthy body.

The arrangement suited Mma-Tselane. She was big-hearted and broad-minded and yet, conversely, she prided herself in being the meticulous upholder of all the traditions the community adhered to. Once Mma-Monosi became a part of the household, Mma-Tselane did no work but entertained and paid calls the day long. Mma-Monosi ran the entire household.

The two women complemented each other, for, if Mma-Tselane was a queen, then Mma-Monosi was a humble worker. On the surface, Mma-Monosi appeared as sane and balanced as Mma-Tselane, but there was another side to her personality that was very precariously balanced. Mma-Monosi took her trembling way through life. If all was stable and peaceful, then Mma-Monosi was stable and peaceful. If there was any disruption or disorder, Mma-Monosi's precarious inner balance registered every wave and upheaval. She hungered for approval of her every action and could be upset for days if criticised or reprimanded.

So, between them, the two women achieved a very harmonious household. Both were entirely absorbed in their full busy daily round; both were unconcerned that they received scant attention from the man of the household and Rra-Tselane was entirely concerned with his own affairs. He was a prominent member of the chief's court and he divided his time between the chief's court and his cattle-post. He was rich in cattle and his herds were taken care of by servants. He was away at his cattle-post at that time.

It was with Mma-Monosi that the young girl, Tselane, enjoyed a free and happy relationship. They treated each other as equals both enjoyed hard work and whenever they were alone together, they laughed and joked all the time. Her own mother regarded Tselane as an object to whom she lowered her voice and issued commands between clenched teeth. Very soon Mma-Tselane stirred in her chair and said in that lowered voice: 'Tselane, fetch me my bag of herbs.'

Tselane obediently stood up and hurried to her mother's living quarters for the bag of herbs. Another interval followed during which her mother and the visitor discussed the medicinal properties of the herbs. Then Mma-Monosi served the evening meal. Before long the visitor departed with assurances that Mma-Tselane would call on her the following day. Then they sat for a while in companionable silence. At one stage, seeing that the fire was burning low, Mma-Tselane arose and selected a few pieces of wood from Tselane's bundle to stoke up the fire.

'Er, Tselane', she said, 'your wood is quite dry. Did you shelter from the storm?

'There is a cave in the hill not far from here, mother', Tselane replied. 'And I sheltered there.' She did not think it was wise to add that she had sheltered with a young man, a lot of awkward questions of the wrong kind might have followed.

The mother cast her eyes vaguely over her daughter as if to say all was in order in her world; she always established simple facts about any matter and turned peacefully to the next task at hand. She suddenly decided that she was tired and would retire. Tselane and Mma-Monosi were left alone seated near the fire. Tselane was still elated by her encounter with the young man; so many pleasant thoughts were flying through her head.

'I want to ask you some questions, Mma-Monosi', she said, eagerly.

'What is it you want to say, my child?' Mma-Monosi said, stirring out of a reverie.

'Do you approve of arranged marriages, Mma-Monosi?' she asked, earnestly.

Mma-Monosi drew in her breath between her teeth with a sharp, hissing sound, then she lowered her voice in horror and said:

'Tselane, you know quite well that I am your friend but if anyone else heard you talking like that you would be in trouble! Such things are never discussed here! What put that idea into your head because it is totally unknown to me.'

'But you question life when you begin to grow up', Tselane said defensively.

'That is what you never, never do', Mma-Monosi said severely. 'If you question life you will upset it. Life is always in order.' She looked thoroughly startled and agitated. 'I know of something terrible that once happened to someone who questioned life', she added grimly.

'Who is this? What terrible thing happened?' Tselane asked in her turn agitated.

'I can't tell you', Mma-Monosi said firmly. 'It is too terrible to mention.'

Tselane subsided into silence with a speculative look in her eye. She understood Mma-Monosi well. She couldn't keep a secret. She could always be tempted into telling a secret, if not today then on some other day. She decided to find out the terrible story.

When Keaja arrived home his family was eating the evening meal. He first approached the women's quarters and offered them the gourd of milk.

'The cows are calving heavily', he explained. 'There is a lot of milk and I can bring some home every day.'

He was greeted joyously by the second and third wives of his father who anxiously enquired after their sons who lived with him at the cattle-post.

'They are quite well', he said, politely. 'I settled them and the cattle before I left. I shall return again in the early morning because I am worried about the young calves.'

He avoided his mother's baleful stare and tight, deprived mouth. She never had anything to say to him, although, on his approach to the women's quarters, he had heard her voice, shrill and harsh, dominating the conversation. His meal was handed to him and he retreated to his father's quarters. He ate alone and apart from the women. A bright fire burned in his father's hut.

'Hullo, Father-of-Me', his father greeted him, making affectionate play on the name Keaja which means I am eating now because I have a son to take care of me.

His father doted on him. In his eyes there was no greater son than Keaja. After an exchange of greetings his father asked:

'And what is your news?'

He gave his father the same information about the cows calving heavily and the rich supply of milk; that his other two sons were quite well. They ate for a while in companionable silence. His mother's voice rose shrill and penetrating in the silent night. Quite unexpectedly his father looked up with a twinkle in his eye and said:

'Those extra calves will stand us in good stead, Father-of-Me. I have just started negotiations about your marriage.'

A spasm of chill, cold fear almost constricted Keaja's

91

heart.

'Who am I to marry, father?' he asked, alarmed.

'I cannot mention the family name just yet', his father replied, cheerfully, not sensing his son's alarm. 'The negotiations are still at a very delicate stage.'

'Have you committed yourself in this matter, father?' he asked, a sharp angry note in his voice.

'Oh yes', his father replied. 'I have given my honour in this matter. It is just that these things take a long time to arrange as there are many courtesies to be observed.'

'How long?' Keaja asked.

'About six new moons may have to pass', his father replied. 'It may even be longer than that. I cannot say at this stage.'

'I could choose a wife for myself.' the son said, with deadly quietude. 'I could choose my own wife and then inform you of my choice.'

His father stared at him in surprise.

'You cannot be different from everyone else', he said. 'I must be a parent with a weakness that you can talk to me so.'

Keaja lowered his eyes to his eating bowl. There was no way in which he could voice a protest against his society because the individual was completely smothered by communal and social demands. He was a young man possessed by individual longings and passions; he had a nervous balance that either sought complete isolation or true companionship and communication and for a long while all appeared in order with him because of the deceptive surface peace of his personality. Even that evening Keaja's protest against an arranged marriage was hardly heard by his father.

His father knew that he indulged his son, that they had free and easy exchanges beyond what was socially permissible; even that brief exchange was more than all parents allowed their children. They arranged all details of their children's future and on the fatal day merely informed them that they were to be married to so-and-so. There was no point in saying: 'I might not be able to live with so-and-so. She might be unsuited to me', so that when Keaja lapsed into silence, his father merely smiled indulgently and engaged him in small talk.

Keaja was certainly of marriageable age. The previous year he had gone through his initiation ceremony. Apart from other trials endured during the ceremony, detailed instruction had been given to the young men of his age group about sexual relations between men and women. They were hardly private and personal but affected by a large number of social regulations and taboos. If he broke the taboos at a personal and private level, death, sickness and great misfortune would fall upon his family. If he broke the taboos at a social level, death and disaster would fall upon the community.

There were many periods in a man's life when abstinence from sexual relations was required; often this abstinence had to be practised communally as in the period preceding the harvest of crops and only broken on the day of the harvest thanksgiving ceremony.

These regulations and taboos applied to men and women alike but the initiation ceremony for women, which Tselane had also experienced the previous year, was much more complex in its instruction. A delicate balance had to be preserved between a woman's reproductive cycle and the safety of the community; at almost every stage in her life a woman was a potential source of danger to the community. All women were given careful instruction in precautions to be observed during times of menstruation, childbirth and accidental miscarriages. Failure to observe the taboos could bring harm to animal life, crops and the community.

It could be seen then that the community held no place for people wildly carried away by their passions, that there was logic and order in the carefully arranged sterile emotional and physical relationships between men and women. There was no one to challenge the established order of things; if people felt any personal unhappiness it was smothered and subdued and so life for the community proceeded from day to day in peace and harmony.

As all lovers do, they began a personal and emotional dialogue that excluded all life around them. Perhaps its pattern and direction was the same for all lovers, painful and maddening by turns in its initial insecurity.

Who looked for who? They could not say, except that the far-western unpolluted end of the river where women drew water and the forests where they gathered firewood became Keaja's favourite hunting grounds. Their work periods coincided at that time. The corn had just been sown and the women were idling in the village until the heavy soaking rains raised the weeds in their fields, then their next busy period would follow when they hoed out the weeds between their corn.

Keaja returned every day to the village with gourds of milk for his family and it did not take Tselane long to note that he delayed and lingered in her work areas until he had caught some glimpse of her. She was always in a crowd of gaily chattering young women. The memory of their first encounter had been so fresh and stimulating, so full of unexpected surprises in dialogue that she longed to approach him.

One afternoon, while out gathering wood with her companions, she noticed him among the distant bushes and contrived to remove herself from her companions. As she walked towards him, he quite directly approached her and took hold of her hand. She made no effort to pull her hand free. It rested in his as though it belonged there. They walked on some distance, then he paused, and turning to face her told her all he had on his mind in his direct, simple way. This time he did not smile at all.

'My father will arrange a marriage for me after six new moons have passed', he said. 'I do not want that. I want a wife of my own choosing but all the things I want can only cause trouble.'

She looked away into the distance not immediately knowing what she ought to say. Her own parents had given her no clue of their plans for her future; indeed she had not had cause to think about it but she did not like most of the young men of the village. They had a hang-dog air as though the society and its oppressive ways had broken their will. She liked everything about Keaja and she felt safe with him as on that stormy afternoon in the cavern when he had said: 'We can shelter here together from the storm . . .'

'My own thoughts are not complicated', he went on, still holding on to her hand. 'I thought I would find out how you felt about this matter. I thought I would like to choose you as my wife. If you do not want to choose me in turn, I shall not pursue my own wants any longer. I might even marry the wife my father chooses for me.'

She turned around and faced him and spoke with a clarity of thought that startled her.

'I am afraid of nothing', she said. 'Not even trouble or death, but I need some time to find out what I am thinking.'

Het let go of her hand and so they parted and went their separate ways. From that point onwards right until the following day, she lived in a state of high elation. Her thought processes were not all coherent, indeed she had not a thought in her head. Then the illogic of love took over. Just as she was about to pick up the pitcher in the late afternoon, she suddenly felt desperately ill, so ill that she was almost brought to the point of death. She experienced a paralysing lameness in her arms and legs. The weight of the pitcher with which she was to draw water was too heavy for her to endure.

She appealed to Mma-Monosi.

'I feel faint and ill today', she said. 'I cannot draw water.'

Mma-Monosi was only too happy to take over her chores but at the same time consulted anxiously with her mother about this sudden illness. Mma-Tselane, after some deliberation, decided that it was the illness young girls get when they are growing too rapidly.

She spent a happy three days doctoring her daughter with warm herb drinks as Mma-Tselane liked nothing better than to concentrate on illness. Still, the physical turmoil the young girl felt continued unabated; at night she trembled violently from head to toe. It was so shocking and new that for two days she succumbed completely to the blow. It wasn't any coherent thought processes that made her struggle desperately to her feet on the third day but a need to quieten the anguish. She convinced her mother and Mma-Monosi that she felt well enough to perform her wood gathering chores. Towards the afternoon she hurried to the forest area, carefully avoiding her companions.

She was relieved, on meeting Keaja, to see that his face bore the same anguished look that she felt. He spoke first. 'I felt so ill and disturbed', he said. 'I could do nothing but wait for your appearance.'

They sat down on the ground together. She was so exhausted by her two-day struggle that for a moment she leaned forward and rested her head on his knee. Her thought processes seemed to awaken once more because she smiled contentedly and said: 'I want to think.'

Eventually she raised herself and, with shining eyes, looked at the young man.

'I felt so ill', she said. 'My mother kept on giving me herb drinks. She said it was normal to feel faint and dizzy when one is growing. I know now what made me feel so ill. I was fighting my training. My training has told me that people are not important in themselves but you so suddenly became important to me, as a person. I did not know how to tell my mother all this. I did not know how to tell her anything yet she was kind and took care of me. Eventually I thought I would lose my mind so I came here to find you . . .'

It was as if, from that moment onwards, they quietly and of their own will had married. They began to plan together how and when they should meet.

The young man was full of forethought and planning. He knew that, in terms of his own society, he was starting a terrible mess; but then his society only calculated along the lines of human helplessness in the face of overwhelming odds. It did not calculate for human inventiveness and initiative. He only needed the young girl's pledge and from then onwards he took the initiative in all things. He was to startle and please her from that very day with his logical mind. It was as if he knew that she would come at some time, that they would linger in joy with their love-making, so that when Tselane eventually expressed agitation at the lateness of the hour, he, with a superior smile, indicated a large bundle of wood nearby that he had collected for her to take home.

A peaceful interlude followed and the community innocently lived out its day-by-day life, unaware of the disruption and upheaval that would soon fall upon it. The women were soon out in the fields, hoeing weeds and tending their crops, Tselane among them. She worked side by side with Mma-Monosi, as she had always done. There was not even a ripple of the secret life she now lived; if anything, she worked harder and with greater contentment. She laughed and joked as usual with Mma-Monosi but sound instinct made her keep her private affairs to herself.

When the corn was already high in the fields and about to ripen, Tselane realised that she was expecting a child. A matter that had been secret could be a secret no longer. When she confided this news to Keaja, he quite happily accepted it as a part of all the plans he had made, for as he said to her at that time: 'I am not planning for death when we are so happy. I want that we should live.'

He had only one part of all his planning secure, a safe escape route outside the village and on to a new and unknown life they would make together. They had made themselves outcasts from the acceptable order of village life and he presented her with two plans from which she could choose. The first alternative was the simpler for them. They could leave the village at any moment and without informing anyone of their intentions. The world was very wide for a man. He had travelled great distances, both alone and in the company of other men, while on his hunting and herding duties. The area was safe for travel for some distance. He had sat around firesides and heard stories about wars and fugitives and hospitable tribes who lived far away and whose customs differed from theirs. Keaja had not been idle all this while; he had prepared all they would need for their journey and hidden their provisions in a safe place.

The second alternative was more difficult for the lovers. They could inform their parents of their love and ask that they be married. He was not sure of the outcome but it was to invite death or worse. It might still lead to the escape route out of the village as he was not planning for death.

So after some thought Tselane decided to tell her parents because, as she pointed out, the first plan would be too heart-breaking for their parents. They, therefore, decided on that very day to inform their parents of their love and name the date on which they wished to marry.

It was nearing dusk when Tselane arrived home with her bundle of wood. Her mother and Mma-Monosi were seated out in the courtyard, engaged in some quiet conversation.

Tselane set down her bundle, approached the two women and knelt down quietly by her mother's side. Her mother turned towards her, expecting some request or message from a friend. There was no other way except for Tselane to convey her own message in the most direct way possible.

'Mother', she said. 'I am expecting a child by the son of Rra-Keaja. We wish to be married by the next moon. We love each other . . .'

For a moment her mother frowned as though her child's words did not make sense. Mma-Monosi's body shuddered several times as though she were cold but she maintained a deathly silence. Eventually, Tselane's mother lowered her voice and said between clenched teeth:

'You are to go to your hut and remain there. On no account are you to leave without the supervision of Mma-Monosi.'

For a time Mma-Tselane sat looking into the distance, a broken woman. Her social prestige, her kingdom, her self-esteem crumbled around her.

A short while later her husband entered the yard. He had spent an enjoyable day at the chief's court with other men. He now wished for his evening meal and retirement for the night. The last thing he wanted was conversation with women, so he looked up irritably as his wife appeared without his evening meal. She explained herself with as much dignity as she could muster. She was almost collapsing with shock. He listened in disbelief and gave a sharp exclamation of anger.

'Tselane', Mma-Monosi said, earnestly. 'It is no light matter to break custom. You pay for it with your life. I should have told you the story that night we discussed custom. When I was a young girl we had a case such as this but not such a deep mess. The young man had taken a fancy to a girl and she to him. He, therefore, refused the girl his parents had chosen for him. They could not break him and so they killed him. They killed him even though he had not touched the girl. But there is one thing I want you to know. I

98

am your friend and I will die for you. No one will injure you while I am alive.'

Their easy, affectionate relationship returned to them. They talked for some time about the love affair, Mma-Monosi absorbing every word with delight. A while later Mma-Tselane re-entered the yard. She was still too angry to talk to her own child but she called Mma-Monosi to one side and informed her that she had won an assurance in high places that no harm would come to her child.

And so began a week of raging storms and wild irrational deliberations. It was a family affair. It was a public affair. As a public affair it would bring ruin and disaster upon the community and public anger was high. Two parents showed themselves up in a bad light, the father of Tselane and the mother of Keaja. Rra-Tselane was adamant that the marriage would never take place. He preferred to sound death warnings all the time. The worm that had been eating at the heart of Keaja's mother all this while finally arose and devoured her heart. She too could be heard to sound death warnings. Then a curious and temporary solution was handed down from high places. It was said that if the lovers removed themselves from the community for a certain number of days, it would make allowance for public anger to die down. Then the marrigae of the lovers would be considered.

So appalling was the drama to the community that on the day Keaja was released from his home and allowed to approach the home of Tselane, all the people withdrew to their own homes so as not to witness the fearful sight. Only Mma-Monosi, who had supervised the last details of the departure, stood openly watching the direction in which the young lovers left the village. She saw them begin to ascend the hill not far from the home of Tselane. As darkness was approaching, she turned and walked back to her yard. To Mma-Tselane, who lay in a state of nervous collapse in her hut, Mma-Monosi made her last, sane pronouncement on the whole affair.

'The young man is no fool', she said. 'They have taken the direction of the hill. He knows that the hilltop is superior to any other. People are angry and someone might think of attacking them. An attacker will find it a difficult task as the young man will hurl stones down on him before he ever gets near. Our child is quite safe with him.'

Then the story took a horrible turn. Tension built up towards the day the lovers were supposed to return to community life. Days went by and they did not return. Eventually search parties were sent out to look for them but they had disappeared. Not even their footmarks were visible on the bare rock faces and tufts of grass on the hillside. At first the searchers returned and did not report having seen any abnormal phenomena, only a baffled surprise. Then Mma-Monosi's precarious imaginative balance tipped over into chaos. She was seen walking grief-stricken towards the hill. As she reached its base she stood still and the whole drama of the disappearance of the lovers was re-created before her eyes. She first heard loud groans of anguish that made her blood run cold. She saw that as soon as Tselane and Keaja set foot on the hill, the rocks parted and a gaping hole appeared. The lovers sank into its depths and the rocks closed over them. As she called, 'Tselane! Keaja!' their spirits rose and floated soundlessly with unseeing eyes to the top of the hill.

Mma-Monosi returned to the village and told a solemn and convincing story of all she had seen. People only had to be informed that such phenomena existed and they all began seeing it too. Then Mma-Tselane, maddened and distraught by the loss of her daughter slowly made her way to the hill. With sorrowful eyes she watched the drama re-create itself before her. She returned home and died.

The hill from then onwards became an unpleasant embodiment of sinister forces which destroyed life. It was no longer considered a safe dwelling place for the tribe. They packed up their belongings on the backs of their animals, destroyed the village and migrated to a safer area.

The deserted area remained unoccupied until 1875 when people of the Bamalete tribe settled there. Although strangers to the area, they saw the same phenomenon, heard the loud groans of anguish and saw the silent floating spirits of the lovers. The legend was kept alive from generation to generation and so the hill stands to this day in the village of Otse in southern Botswana as an eternal legend of love. Letswe La Baratani. The Hill of the Lovers.

The General

The President and Saviour of the people paced up and down the thickly carpeted floor, plunged in meditation. Now and then he stopped and admired the graceful line of his long slender feet which were shod in brown sandals of fine leather. He raised his hands too and admired their smooth black colour and the dark criss-cross lines on his large wide palms.

'What strong hands I have!', he said and laughed at himself affectionately. And there was no one nearby to check the laughter because, for some time now, he had surrounded himself entirely with an entourage who felt a mystical reverence for his person.

People are unreasonable. They had elected him their leader and Saviour on a tide of wild enthusiasm and after a time it became difficult to reject a God they themselves had created. The times had changed too. Over the centuries of terror and persecution people had, unknown to themselves, grown brave and every sign of coercion awoke a vengeful passion in their hearts. To the battery of propaganda from all sides, they responded with silent cynical distrust. The nature of Gods had changed too. They had become ordinary men in an ordinary world where none could set himself up as superior to his fellow men.

Things were not so bad in the beginning. The President had charm and his intellectual brilliance was recognised throughout the whole world. He was completely objective and that was his charm. That is why when he said:

'I am the composite type of all the dictators of the world ...' the statement was regarded as strikingly original; he created the effect that he was the distant scholar reflecting on the dictators of the world. He had a warm engaging manner when speaking to close associates. After outlining a proposal with dazzling clarity, he would turn to an admirer:

'What do you think, Bill?'

It was only remarked upon, after a succession of brilliant

young men were detained or forced into exile, that he invariably surrounded himself with men of dull wit or mediocre intellect.

There was M.M. Makhudo who drew up the first Five Year Plan which resulted in an economic and industrial boom. A month after the plan was published, a daily paper carried a thoughtful assessment of his work. A few days later Makhudo lost his job on the government planning group. The word was passed around that he was an exhibitionist, a self-seeking egoist. In the new society there were to be no personalities but servants of the people dedicated to the welfare of the people. In a new society there are so many many Makhudo's to be got rid of and that is called doing-what-ought-to-be-done; clearing the way so that only the good people are left.

The official opposition to the government was not much good. Given half the chance they would have assassinated half the citizens in the country as they were always threatening to do. Their language on every crisis *they* invented was wildly abusive:

'You and you and your dirty jackets', was one of their favourite phrases. Even the bitterest critics of the President were agreed that he was justified in locking them up. The people did not complain either. Through all the posturing and breast beating, they saw hard-eyed woman-chasers and greedy speculators. People may be unreasonable in the way they change their mind about their chosen Gods but they are not fools.

To have immortality thrust upon them is a temptation few men can resist. A few months after the President had been elected to office, immortality was offered to him by five priests who called on him during the hour he had set aside for consultation with the public. They aroused his interest with a marvel. One of the priests had the ability to make the whole right side of his body invisible. The President walked around the priest, felt him over carefully, shook him violently and still could not locate the part of his body that seemed to have disappeared into the air.

'You haven't hypnotised me, have you?' he asked sharply.

They said no. They offered to reveal the secret of invisibility, complete physical invisibility to him. He was fascinated, excited at the possibilities this opened to him. And it was true. There was a charm, a simple ritual and behold he was not there! There were other marvels. A chart of complex signs and figures. He was indifferent to this but the words of explanation interested him. The chart traced the life pattern of a great and immortal leader of men, born on the continent, who would yet again change the history of the world. There were certain characteristics; a high degree of intelligence and the choice of a wife from a country foreign to the land of his birth. They spoke with authority and conviction. So they became a part of his household; his destiny too and his Nemesis. They, although in the secluded background of his life, were the directing force of every decision he made. If enemies were eliminated, and there was a succession of them, it was on their advice. A man's enemies have a way of snowballing; especially when there are heaps of bodies in detention camps.

That is how it came to be the General's turn. A pity the soothsayers did not fully grasp the type of personality they were about to come to grips with, because some men have a tough shell they get into at will and from that vantage point no amount of battering can pry them out. They rise above the most appalling circumstances and in a war of nerves they have the stamina to hold out till eternity, if need be. The President, who by this time had become immortal, blanched when the General's name appeared on his elimination list for the day. The loyalty of the army was important to him. But his weird advisers were adamant. There were ill omens surrounding the man. In any case it had become a game — eliminate, eliminate, eliminate until in the end you stand alone, the sole supreme conqueror over a mass of wrecked human lives.

So he called his security chief; a trusted confidante:

'I suspect General Aksan of disloyalty', he said. 'Bring me a full report of his movements, his associates, his activities and his opinions.'

Now he paced up and down, smoothly; unhurriedly. The appointment with the security chief was due to take place in three minutes. It was already settled in his mind that the General was to be dismissed and two weeks previously he had written an urgent letter to the head of another state requesting a replacement for General Aksan. The reply was in the negative. This he considered a gross insult. The head of state he had written to was a close friend. There were possibilities of revenge. He could reveal a closely guarded secret of how that head of state had been the prime engineer of a neat little coup d'état to regain popular favour and at the same time to eliminate, by hanging, seventy powerful enemies at one blow.

'Perhaps he thinks I have lost control of the situation in my own house', the President thought furiously. 'Ishmael has always been a back-stabber. He loves to gloat. I shall revenge him.'

There was a slight sound. A messenger approached, softly, obsequiously, to announce the arrival of the security chief.

'Send him in immediately', the President said.

He put on that wide charming famous smile that had been photographed so often, as the security chief walked in.

'Hullo, Chief', he said warmly, informally. 'You have the report?'

'Yes, sir', the security chief said. He took a yellow file out of his briefcase, handed it over and stood impassively upright.

'Relax, Chief', the President said. 'This will be quite a session. Alienation of the loyalty of the army is no small thing. I have to get the facts straight.'

They settled informally on a long lounge chair. The President opened the file eagerly. It read:

Report on the Activities, Movements,
Opinions & Associates of GENERAL AKSAN,
Chief in Command of the Army.

Activities: Apart from his duties as commander of the army, the General has no extra activities. His work and home life appear to be the centre of his life. Among his confederates at work he is called 'the slave-driver and severe disciplinarian', and is feared. However, a personal trait is discussed with much amusement among confederates. The General is in the habit of walking around with a report sheet in his hand. Should a man of lower rank pass him by, he pretends to be earnestly studying the report. He was once known to have remarked that he disliked being saluted more than was necessary.

Movements: The General adheres to a strict routine. He leaves home at 7.45 a.m. to arrive at work at 8 a.m. His duties cease at 5 p.m. from whence he drives to the Planetaria Hotel. He arrives there at 5.10 and orders two large beers. Exactly at 5.15 he is joined at the bar by Professor Okola, Professor of Economics at the University. Both immediately plunge into deep conversation from which they do not draw their heads until exactly 6 p.m. The General then drives Professor Okola home and arrives at his own home at exactly 6.30 p.m. This he has done for four years, ever since assuming his duties as commander of the army.

Opinions: At work the General has never been known to have a personal opinion on any subject or even to pass idle remarks about the weather. However, a recording was made of one of the engrossing discussions with Professor Okola during their regular evening sessions at the bar of the Planetaria Hotel.

Associates: The aloof manner of the General repels. The only known associates of the General are Professor Okola and his wife.

The report ended. Directly underneath followed a report on Professor Okola:
'He is altogether a strange and fanciful character. At his lectures there are peals of laughter and very little serious study. His air of laxity encourages students to express highly critical opinions about Government and Government personnel. Our revered President himself is often a target of ridicule. Professor Okola indulges in all manner of conversations on deviationist subjects with anyone who will stop and listen to

him for an instant. So engrossed is Professor Okola in conversing and laughter that he leaves his briefcase behind wherever it is he happens to stop and converse. Exam papers have been known to be lost and Professor Okola appears to be permanently afflicted with amnesia. I questioned the administrator of the University about this reckless, exhibitionistic deviationist. He expressed alarm and said he would look into the matter and seriously warn Professor Okola to improve his discipline and memory. The contents of the briefcase which is continuously left about consist of a wide correspondence with Professors of Economics from all parts of the world, the handwritten draft of a manuscript entitled: 'A Comparative Study of Economics', a plan for a students' Marxist Study Group and half-a-dozen half eaten packets of peppermints.'

The President sprang to his feet, the file still in his hand. There was something in the report on the General that agitated him, destroyed his air of calm unhurried composure. The security chief misunderstood the cause of his agitation.

'About Professor Okola, Sir', he began. 'I have at least twenty witnesses . . .'

The President laughed, regaining his composure.

'Oh that exhibitionistic fool', he said affectionately. 'So Africa too, has its version of the absent-minded professor. It's a universal phenomenon, Chief. When the thought processes are geared to a certain level of intensity, the individual becomes oblivious to his surroundings. Besides, we are a mature government. It's a healthy sign if the Professor encourages students to exercise their critical faculties. No, no, Chief. It's the sinister character of this awe-inspiring General 'Ironsides' that troubles me. See that man-to-man touch? On the one hand, aloof, unapproachable. On the other, the cynical gesture — even though I am above you, still I am one of you. I am not a demi-god to be saluted on every occasion. This is the character of an opportunist driven by a ruthless lust for power. 'Ironsides' has the army eating out of his hand and in an unstable situation what's to stop him from making a bid for the power he so obviously craves night and day? Ah, I have the perfect plan to break the will of this opportunist.

Let us hear what these two great friends discuss each evening with such intense concentration.'

The efficient security chief took a small compact box from his briefcase. There was a click and the slow deep voice of General Akson startled the two men as though his live presence was with them. He said:

'. . . As you were saying last night, Okola. You are in doubt about the value of human rights.'

The soft diffident voice of the Professor replied:

'What rights ought a man to expect, Aksan? After these years of liberation, what do we have here? Such a smug lot among the upper crust with a contempt for the ordinary man; a government we distrust and a pack of roaming roughnecks who say: If you say one word against the government, we will murder you. Aksan, I am weary of all the enemies of Africa, imaginary or real; I am weary of the futility of fear and suffering and I am weary of being an African and all that it means.'

There was a deep chuckle from the General.

'If you had your way, Okola, you would stop the stream of life altogether. A man must keep his sights down and not live up in the air as you do. For some, suffering is most welcome and when faced with death or danger they are as hard as stone. Would you deny them what is their greatest joy in life simply because suffering appears futile to you?'

The Professor sounded slightly offended.

'I don't like the way you picture me as an idle metaphysical romantic with my head in the clouds. Why do I strain myself with a comparative study of economics? It is because millions of people suffer from hunger. You say to yourself: Is poverty then such an unwieldy problem? I hope that my conclusions can be added to that great army of thinkers all over the world who are trying day and night to alleviate this condition. That is why, when I have completed my studies, I am going to persuade you to remove your uniform and till the earth with me. Has it ever occurred to you, Aksan, that you are the walking image of a murderer?'

The General laughed loudly.

'I never quite pictured myself that way, Okola. How

108

strangely different we are from each other in preference. I once read somewhere that men who are troubled with their gall bladders are of a quarrelsome temperament. It might be possible that men with gall bladder trouble evolved the first system of warfare because they just can't stand peace. How can I give up my uniform for a peaceful pursuit like agriculture? I have a preference for it and am troubled with my gall bladder.'

There was joint laughter. The Professor said:

'Well, well. Up to date that is the most original defence I have yet heard for murder. But . . .'

The President waved his hand. He had heard enough and was ready to make his pronouncements.

'The Professor', he said, 'seems uncertain as to whether he is dead or alive. He flounders around in a morass of idle revisionist thought. To help him clarify his ideas, while under preventive detention, he is to read my book on the socio-economic political philosophy for the new Africa. That ought to give him a coherent base for future discussions. The General is to be dismissed on arrival for duty at 8 a.m. tomorrow. I shall assume the position of supreme commander of the army. The General is to be prevented from obtaining alternative employment and prevented from leaving the capital city. By creating these frustrating circumstances I wish to force his hand. He is sure to start an intrigue. Although most of our comrades are gutless cowards and turn tail on a man when the wind blows the wrong way for him, the reckless Professor will rush over to his friend. He is to be arrested as he leaves the General's house. Should he interfere with the arrest of the Professor, clobber him but don't shoot or injure to kill. The arrest of the Professor is to frighten off would-be sympathisers. I want the General to move out and make the first approach. To use a cliché, we are giving the General enough rope to hang himself.'

Professor Okola first heard of the dismissal of his friend when he entered the canteen during the lunch hour. For the rest of the day he felt ill and distracted. Of course, such things were almost a daily occurrence. Men in high positions suddenly disappeared from public life. The whole country was divided. There were those, loud and vociferous in their support of every government decision and the vast silent majority with few illusions left about the price one had to pay to resist tyranny. Friendship and the knowledge of the worth of a man shrank into insignificance before such a mountain of tyranny. He was too distracted to teach and gave his students an essay to write. Unconsciously he paced up and down wringing his hands. The students bent their heads pretending not to notice. He was the most popular lecturer. It was already near sunset when he was free. He immediately left for the General's house.

Their friendship was a rare and harmonious one. On the one hand the Professor had come to take the calm solid presence of the General almost like a medicine. He was a high-strung, nervous man, afflicted by the odd minor ailments of a nervous temperament — a sudden lameness in the arms; a sudden abrupt cessation of energy. Often, when faced with a crisis, his lips trembled uncontrollably. The General radiated solid peace and strength. On the other hand, the General was conscious of the narrowness of his interests. A horizon, wide and open, had to be revealed to him and Professor Okola was interested in *everything*.

That evening General Aksan sat in his lounge reading. There was an urgent knock. His wife opened the door and Professor Okola rushed in. He looked the picture of anxiety.

The General smiled. He said:

'You ought not to have come here, my friend. There is a deeper motive in this. Why am I not detained like all the rest?'

The Professor drew himself up proudly.

'Aksan, I have a little investment and it is called individual freedom. No man, unless he chains me, can prevent me from visiting you.'

He sat down. The General's wife removed herself quietly to prepare some refreshments. She was a shy self-effacing woman with a long thin pensive face. They had no children.

Professor Okola said:

'What are your plans now, Aksan?'

'I don't quite know, Okola', he said. 'However, today I

found a book on gardening among my small collection. I thought to myself: One day I might have to till the earth with Okola but agriculture is too vast a subject for me to grasp in middle age. Perhaps gardening would do just as well and I have a wide enclosed space in my backyard.'

Professor Okola laughed.

'And to think Aksan, just the other day I said I would have to persuade you to remove your uniform. Now it has been forcibly removed. In civilian clothes you are indeed a humble-looking fellow. Yes, certainly events are ahead of us.'

'It seems to me as though there is a logic in events', the General said.

The Professor looked at his friend thoughtfully.

'We live in a torrent of evil. Perhaps you are right. There is more logic in evil events than good. You almost feel an end in sight somewhere; a catalytic end. What was the cause of your dismissal, Aksan?'

'I am suspected of disloyalty', the General said.

He paused awhile then continued musingly:

'Africa', he said. 'A continent where men are contained because they are rivulets of molten fire and those who do the containing have themselves in turn to be contained. Just say there is a volcano here. Can a volcano be contained when the time has come for it to erupt? A fanciful idea? Why do we so profoundly distrust each other? Why do we so profoundly fear competition from each other? It seems to me that in some dim and ancient past of our history, bedlam reigned. Men must have been wild and riotous and free and long ago this was condemned. The system of suppression is so ancient here.'

Professor Okola was alarmed.

'Oh, Aksan', he said. 'It grieves me to hear you talk this way. You are not a philosopher but a man of action. This is so unlike you.'

'Can't a man of action prepare himself for solitude, Okola?'

The General's wife brought in some refreshment. The rest of the time was spent in silence. Because of the shock the two friends felt an unease and heavy foreboding.

111

Just as Professor Okola lifted his hand off the gate and waved a last greeting to the solitary figure of the General standing in the shadow of the porch, two uniformed figures sprang out of the dark and grasped him roughly by both arms. He heard the harsh command; a swift movement and the deep grave voice of the General:

'Let go of him or kill me.'

The Professor's heart thudded painfully.

'Aksan', he said sharply. 'This is none of your business. Do not interfere.'

They removed the Professor. For a long hour the General stood rooted to the spot, lost in an eclipse of silent, violent rage. When he entered the house his wife pretended she had not been crying. She feared it might seem a weakness and weakness, any weakness was what he despised most of all.

Two days later university students demonstrated outside the palatial mansion of the President for the release of Professor Okola from preventive detention. It was said the students were rioting and the police came out in full force, some skulls were broken and a large number of students jailed. This provided the President with an excuse to have an immense two-walled brick barricade built around his mansion. The news that the army had signed a petition refusing to accept him as their commander-in-chief was carefully suppressed. Then the people saw two hundred strange foreign guards on duty outside the President's mansion. However, things seemed to go on much as before. Only foreign intriguers, as they were called, kept printing news items that the economy of the country had reached inflation stage and was near bankruptcy. But this could be easily denied. There was a Mercedes Benz on every corner.

The General seemed to be a forgotten man. It seemed as though he had imposed a form of house arrest on himself. The backyard of his home gradually took on the shape of a luxuriant tropical garden. So a year and two months passed.

On a cool still tropical winter afternoon there were sudden shouts and a scurrying of terrified feet. Shots and shouts; stones and broken glass became a repeated pattern of sound throughout the four hours of that cool winter afternoon.

But the General continued reading. His wife quietly embroidered a table cloth.

Towards evening there was an urgent knock on the door. The General opened it. A group of five army officers walked in. They arranged themselves in file and saluted briskly. A spokesman for the group explained that they had overthrown the government and had come to ask him to be the head of a new army government. He said nothing. Yet he climbed the stairs to his bedroom. Moments later he re-appeared in uniform, dressed to the last braid and button. That silent magnificent masculine gesture of exquisite dignity was the only affirmation he gave to them of his willingness to head the new government.

It was near midnight of the same day when an army vehicle drew up outside the detention camp. No one was asleep and it seemed as though thousands and thousands of prisoners were being ushered in. Professor Okola was horrified and could make nothing out of the sudden incoherent chaos. It seemed like Judgement Day with all the weeping, wailing and gnashing of teeth. He was still more horrified when his name was called and he was driven through the streets. The vehicle's light picked out bodies everywhere lying in pools of blood.

'What happened?' he asked.

'We had a revolution', one of the officers replied.

The Professor's lips trembled. He had never visualised the wreckage of blood and bodies.

'Where are you taking me?' he asked. It seemed at last that if death awaited him, he would find welcome relief in it.

'Your friend, the General, asked for you', the officer again replied. 'He is head of the new government.'

The Professor was struck speechless. Aksan, a politician? Aksan, the administrator of this chaos? He busied his mind with an argument. Perhaps there was still time; quick, quick, quick; a way to pull Aksan out of this arena of hate and intrigue and greed and vengeance.

But when he came face to face with his friend, his hopes fell to the ground. There was only endless despair. The black eyes of his friend were lit up with the fierce exhilarating light

113

of victory. There was much saluting and the click-click of heels as army officers streamed in and out of the General's office. Professor Okola took in the scene in a daze of despair.

At last the General waved his hand, closed the door and they were alone. He looked at his friend appraisingly and laughed loudly.

'Okola, my friend', he said. 'You are shaking like a jelly-fish.'

Still the Professor was speechless. The General roared with laughter.

'I know you so well, Okola. You are thinking: Has Aksan, too become one of the tyrannical despots? Well, you ought to know me well enough. I am here first and foremost because I have a preference for power but over and above that we had a society that almost died through the greed and tyranny of a few men. It is you, Okola, who has cried loudly for a better society and now that you are in a position to strike a blow in the name of truth and justice, you stand there desperately praying that the stream of life should stop.'

'You cannot force me to be a politician', the Professor said vehemently.

'Okola, you are an anarchist; a dangerous radical anarchist. Do you think for one moment I would allow you to wander about freely to heap scorn and ridicule on the government? Why, you alone can create a counter-revolution in six days! But seriously, my friend, I need you. Without you I am lost. In the heat of the moment and in disgust at the practices of the former government I announced that there would be free economic enterprise for everyone and already I am being denounced throughout the continent as the paid puppet of Washington. Not that that bothers me. The trouble here is a bankrupt country. All those crooks have salted away the money. I am recalling M.M. Makhudo from exile tomorrow and if you wish you may work with him on the economic planning group. We need so much, Okola, and the safeguards against the repetition of the faults of the former government are not there. I am not the government alone and there are thousands of crooks awaiting their turn to live off the people's blood like leeches and people do not yet fully grasp the

114

concerted power of their will to resist evil. They accept tyranny in silence and wait for one man to oppose it.'

The Professor felt trapped. He could not leave his friend alone in this dangerous world.

'Just promise me, Aksan', he said slowly. 'Just promise me that one day soon, we shall leave all this and till the earth together.'

Son of the Soil

Each generation lived in its own time and each generation knew nothing of the afflictions endured by the preceding generations. But the downward slide into hopeless slavery had unfolded with rhythmic calculation since the time the white man first set foot on the land. So dark and evil was the history of the land that the true details of oppression were never recorded.

The missionaries, who pioneered their services among the tribes, initially said kind things. They said that when the Romans first took learning to the tribes of Europe, the tribes there were still like the tribes of South Africa, not knowing anything of learning and progress. The missionaries had come to bring learning and upliftment to the people.

'We are really taking the bull by the horns this time', the people said, in wonderment at the new learning. 'The white man is old in wisdom.'

Life was easeful at that time. Men owned huge herds of cattle. They also hunted and brayed and prepared wild animal skins for clothes and shoes. Their cattle grazed in green valleys and the cattle-herds dozed in the noon-day heat under the shade of trees. People only murmured at the disparagement in values between themselves and the foreign invaders. The foreign invaders had a fever for 'pretty coloured stones' and golden metal that was dug out from the deep bowels of the earth. They could not understand this fever for diamonds and gold which had no utilitarian value.

'Iron is probably better than all those things', they said. 'We have made hoes and spears and axes from it since the beginning of time. It is a knowledge that came from our race.'

Little remained in the memory of this early period. The gold and diamond exploration concession documents all bore the small mark of an illiterate chieftain. Brandy flowed like water over this period — some of the land was sold for drink, some for mutual friendship and some by trickery and fraud.

Once the land had been securely wrested from the people, 'white man's drink' became for a century, a superior intoxicant unsuited for consumption by the 'kaffirs'.

Ownership of the land changed hands swiftly. The alarmed murmurs of the people went unheeded:

'We have agreed to give certain white men farms in our country – those who have helped us, those who have lived with us, those who have fought for us. These men are known to us and we can bear witness concerning them at any time. These gifts of farms and their title deeds are not things which can be bought according to our custom. Our meaning was that they live there and plough there. They have sold the land for money. We ask that they return the money to those who have given out money . . .'

These protests were made, not in places of power, but in the traditional way by night-time fireside places. They were ridiculous because they never reached the ears of the nations of Europe who began to carve up the continent of Africa for their own use. More often, single white men became owners of vast tracts of land and the tribes became squatters or tenants on this land. In their new position as squatters or tenants, people ploughed their land as usual, but on harvesting their crops they handed over fifty per cent of the harvest as tithes to the new landowner for the privilege of squatting on his land. They humbly accepted their new status.

'We lost the land because we were uneducated and uncivilised', they said.

The 1830s heralded a new era of colonial expansion into the interior of Southern Africa. Formerly, the main area of foreign settlement had been in the Cape Colony. The British and the Dutch or Trek Boer represented conflicting interests in the land. The Boer chafed at the restraints and elegancies of British rule in the Cape Colony. In 1833, the British abolished slavery throughout all their colonies and offered compensation to all former slave owners. The Boer, who had by that time, settled on the back of the black man like a leech, deeply resented the freeing of slaves. In Boer reasoning, so the history books recorded, it had been necessary for the

British to free their slaves because they did not treat their slaves nicely. It had not been necessary for the Boers to free their slaves. A special relationship of understanding existed between Boer and black man. A black man needed to be horse-whipped as a daily natural occurrence in his life; a black man needed to be a servant of a master. A black man had no life beyond that. The Boers began to trek away from the Cape Colony in order to maintain their independent way of life.

In 1852 the Boers set up their first independent Republic in the Transvaal, followed by the Republic of the Orange Free State in 1854. The Cape Colony and the Natal Province became British possessions.

No coloniser was more loved at that time by black people than the British and the Cape Colony became the great centre of culture and learning for black men. Large tracts of land were allocated to black people with planning for future expansion and progress. If imitation is the highest form of flattery, then black men of that time who aspired to learning, modelled themselves on the British way of life. They wore elegant Victorian suits and carried courteous calling cards. They wrote books in the flowery, decorative language of the Victorian era and love, family life and child-rearing were all touched by Victorian sentimentality.

A very different way of life unfolded in the two Boer Republics. The land was wrested from the tribes by conquest and plunder and life was a desolate nightmare of unrelieved horror.

'No Kaffir can own land or cattle in our states', the Boer declared. 'No Kaffir children can receive an education in our states. At the age of fifteen all Kaffir children must enter the service of the white man or be put into prison . . .'

Irrational logic became the order of the day. The Boers built churches, schools and towns for themselves alone, yet the cheap manual labour for towns was provided by black hands. Black men had to be arrested and imprisoned before they realised that a God in a Boer church was not the same universal God come to save black men from their 'heathen ways'. A Boer God in a Boer church was for Boers only.

Timid, docile and broken by violent assertions, black people allowed themselves to be shouted off the pavements of towns they had helped build.

A lot happened in the 1880s. In 1886 the largest gold mine in the world was discovered in the Boer Republic of the Transvaal on the Witwatersrand. It attracted to itself large numbers of adventurers from Britain and Europe who hoped to make their fortunes overnight. They were called 'uitlanders' by the Boers and almost relegated to the status of 'kaffirs', with no franchise rights within the Boer Republic. Partly because of their agitation and partly because the Transvaal Boers opposed free trade between their Republics and the British colonies, the Anglo-Boer war erupted in 1899.

Almost overnight the Boer became the hero of Europe, 'a small, embattled, courageous people' pitting their weight in guerilla warfare against a mighty imperial power. The war progressed with agitation against the British conduct of the war, against the large numbers of Boer women and children detained in concentration camps and the burning of Boer farms. Black bodies silently crept through enemy lines at night delivering messages and despatches from one British command post to another.

'When we realised that the Kaffirs were on the side of the British, then our cause was dark indeed', the Boers said. 'We decided to negotiate peace terms.'

In 1902, the British, who were the victors in the war, began to plan a new society with equal rights and justice for all. The Native of the land shall have the right to vote, they said.

'If the Kaffirs are included in the constitution', the Boer countered. 'We will agitate.'

It was an insignificant matter compared to the major issue of settling Boer and British hostilities and black people were written out of the constitution. The land became known as the Union of South Africa in 1910 and Britain surrendered her possession of the Cape Colony and the Natal Province to the Union government.

Two years went by and then the silent nightmare of horror began. On a day in June 1913, a law was quietly passed in

Parliament by the Union government. It officially declared black people landless:

'No Native shall have the right to hire or purchase farm, grazing or ploughing rights from a landowner. Any land-owner who hires or purchases (sic) farm, grazing or ploughing rights to a Native is subject to a fine of 100 pounds or six month's imprisonment. All Native squatters on white farm land should be immediately evicted with their livestock and consigned to the road immediately the order of eviction is given. Cattle so evicted should remain without food or water till they are sold by their Native owner. A Native may lawfully find employment under a white farmer. Once a wage-earner, a Native's cattle may henceforth work for the landowner, free of charge . . .'

The Act of Parliament read on and on: 'No Native may wander about without a proper pass. A Native's pass must be signed by a white employer to prove he is in legal employ-ment. A Native's basic wage as a farm labourer shall be one shilling per day; a Native's basic wage as a mine labourer shall be one shilling and six pence per day . . .'

The era of the zamindari system of tenant and landowner was abruptly over. One million black people, tenants on the land, wandered the road for six months with their dying stock. On no inch of their own soil could they graze or water their animals. The elegant black men educated in the British liberal tradition, suddenly emerged from the urban centres of Cape Town and Kimberley. They toured the country, collect-ing data on the immense suffering endured by black people under the new law. Their hopes were with Britain and they drew up a manifesto to present to the British Crown.

'We have no representation in Parliament', they said. 'We do not have the right to vote. That right is limited to white men only and we cannot accept the legislation of a parliament that bears no responsibility towards black men . . .'

They nominated amongst themselves a delegation to Britain. Except for the British public, who always loved a cause, the delegation was met with hard-eyed indifference by the powers in control of the British Parliament.

'South Africa is now white man's country', they said. 'We

have been assured that the Natives endure no suffering under the new land act . . .'

There was no hope left except for dispossessed people to offer their cheap labour. And so an era ended and the succeeding generation knew nothing of this matter. It was so shameful that it was never written into the history of the land. History recorded that the South African government was a democratic government, that the early settlers had experienced much harassment from savage chiefs like Dingaan and his Zulu warriors, that Dingaan had put to death two Boers who had peacefully approached him for land rights and in revenge the Boers had destroyed his savage Zulu army. That day was the 16th December 1838 and it shall forever be known as Dingaan's Day.

A period of settlement followed during which white South Africa built up its traditional way of life.

'Our Natives are unlike Natives anywhere else in the world', they said, contentedly. 'They are capable of progress. Once they work for us they will become civilised.'

1948 heralded the triumph of the Boer-dominated Nationalist party and also a new era in the political life of the country — that of organised mass protests, demonstrations and meetings. There was a lot to protest and demonstrate about as one repellent Act after another was passed through parliament and 'apartheid' or rigid segregation of the races became the order of the day. Protest and demonstration availed nothing except that the basic wage was raised from a shilling a day to two pounds per day. Evils were easily written into the laws of the land and an apathy and disillusion settled on the people. It was a world against which there was no hope of appeal.

In 1957 there were faint revived hopes. Ghana was the first country in Africa to gain its independence from a Colonial power and this was rapidly followed by the liberation of all British-held Colonies and Protectorates within the continent. Slowly throughout South Africa, a small, quaint touching gesture was made that seemed to sound a new note of pride and identification with liberated Africa.

For the first time black people evolved a name for themselves of their own choice. They were Africans. Formerly, people had had names imposed on them, to suit the times. Kaffir, which was synonymous to 'heathen' or 'unbeliever', was abandoned when Native was found to be more appropriate. In 1948, Bantu became the official means of address. White-owned newspapers now found themselves consistently bombarded with letters over a long period, compelling them to refer to black people, not as Native or Bantu, but by a name which they preferred — African.

Most black people had become urban communities by that time, living in over-crowded, low-cost municipal settlements outside the big cities and existing to serve the cities with their cheap labour. It was against this background and with a new sense of pride in liberated Africa, that the campaign against the pass book for men was launched on the 21st March 1960.

'We refuse to obey the laws of the land because we have no say in the making of those laws which are imposed on us', was the slogan of the campaign. 'We refuse to carry the pass book any longer . . .'

And people said: 'Why, this is something quite new! It has not been said before! And how right it is!'

They knew nothing of the generation of elegant British-educated black men who had made the same protest on the same terms forty-eight years ago. But, on the appointed day, the men, instead of commuting to work on buses and trains, marched in groups to all the police stations in the land. They laid their pass books down outside the police gates in heaps. As each new group of men joined the groups already assembled, they saluted each other with a quiet greeting:

'Son of the soil', they said.

At about ten o'clock that morning there was a sudden surprised stirring in the crowd of men standing outside a Johannesburg police station. A tall, expensively dressed man quietly joined the crowd. He threw his pass book on the heap and stood staring pensively at the ground. He made no mention of his great deed of the day and the men merely extended to him, the greeting:

'Son of the soil.'

It was only when a few women came rushing towards the police station in excitement that everyone knew of his wonderous gesture. In each municipal house, affixed in one corner, was a small brown box with a single knob. It was the property of the government-owned Radio Bantu Re-diffusion Service. All day long it piped out music and government controlled news. It was too dangerous for black people to own normal radio sets and be in touch with world news, so the knob on the box could either be turned on or turned off. The man was quite well known as the chief announcer of Radio Bantu and, in keeping with his station, he was very highly paid. That morning, instead of announcing the usual government propaganda, he issued a message of his own.

'Women', he said. 'Your men, instead of going to work have gone to the police stations to offer themselves up for a life time of imprisonment rather than carry that hated pass book. The Boers have a monopoly over everything but they still want a monopoly over our minds through this Re-diffusion Service. Tear down those boxes! Pile them up on every street! Burn them!'

And he walked out of Radio Bantu forever. In laughing, chattering groups, the women walked out of their homes with the little boxes on their arms and drew them into heaps on each street corner.

At about eleven o'clock that morning news sped around the country that sixty people had been shot dead outside a police station at Sharpeville. The demonstration had been a peaceful one, and the men outside the Johannesburg police station continued to stare quietly into the distance, in spite of the news. Unexpectedly, from among the crowd, a young man said:

'I think I know why they did it. The Boers always have to spill black blood for any white blood that has been spilled. Last month I was in Cato Manor in Durban where those two Boer police were killed. The Boers were coming around every Sunday and raiding the township for liquor and beer. They would walk around every Sunday and kick over the bottles of brandy and spill the drums of beer, then arrest anyone in sight. They did it that Sunday and they were walking towards their van with a group of men. Suddenly, someone shouted: 'These Boers annoy us every day! We get no peace from them! They make our lives a misery!' Then the people just went mad. They threw the two Boer police to the ground and sat on them. Some of us were indoors eating lunch but we were dragged out of our homes so that all should witness what was done to the Boers. One of the Boers cried: 'Mother, oh my mother, where are you?' His ears were cut off and stuffed into his mouth. The Boers were stabbed over and over again until they were bloody pulp . . .'

The state of emergency, the massive bannings of all political organisations that had acted as a voice for the people, brought to an end the era of mass protests and demonstrations. That era too would no doubt fade from memory because this sort of history was not written into the history of the land.

Footnote:
My historical references for the story were as follows:

Native Life in South Africa, Before and Since the European War and the Boer Rebellion.
by Sol. T. Plaatje (P.S. King & Son Ltd, London 1916. Reprinted by Negro Universities Press, New York 1969).

Austral Africa: Losing It or Ruling It Vols 1 and 11 by John Mackenzie (London 1887, Sampson Low, Marsten & Rivington).

The Prisoner who Wore Glasses

Scarcely a breath of wind disturbed the stillness of the day and the long rows of cabbages were bright green in the sunlight. Large white clouds drifted slowly across the deep blue sky. Now and then they obscured the sun and caused a chill on the backs of the prisoners who had to work all day long in the cabbage field. This trick the clouds were playing with the sun eventually caused one of the prisoners who wore glasses to stop work, straighten up and peer short-sightedly at them. He was a thin little fellow with a hollowed-out chest and comic knobbly knees. He also had a lot of fanciful ideas because he smiled at the clouds.

'Perhaps they want me to send a message to the children,' he thought, tenderly, noting that the clouds were drifting in the direction of his home some hundred miles away. But before he could frame the message, the warder in charge of his work span shouted: 'Hey, what do you think you're doing, Brille?'

The prisoner swung round, blinking rapidly, yet at the same time sizing up the enemy. He was a new warder, named Jacobus Stephanus Hannetjie. His eyes were the colour of the sky but they were frightening. A simple, primitive, brutal soul gazed out of them. The prisoner bent down quickly and a message was quietly passed down the line: 'We're in for trouble this time, comrades.'

'Why?' rippled back up the line.

'Because he's not human', the reply rippled down and yet only the crunching of the spades as they turned over the earth disturbed the stillness.

This particular work span was known as Span One. It was composed of ten men and they were all political prisoners. They were grouped together for convenience as it was one of the prison regulations that no black warder should be in charge of a political prisoner lest this prisoner convert him to his view. It never seemed to occur to the authorities that this very reasoning was the strength of Span One and a clue to the strange terror they aroused in the warders. As political prisoners they were unlike the other prisoners in the sense that they felt no guilt nor were they outcasts of society. All guilty men instinctively cower, which was why it was the kind of prison where men got knocked out cold with a blow at the back of the head from an iron bar. Up until the arrival of Warder Hannetjie, no warder had dared beat any member of Span One and no warder had lasted more than a week with them. The battle was entirely psychological. Span One was assertive and it was beyond the scope of white warders to handle assertive black men. Thus, Span One had got out of control. They were the best thieves and liars in the camp. They lived all day on raw cabbages. They chatted and smoked tobacco. And since they moved, thought and acted as one, they had perfected every technique of group concealment.

Trouble began that very day between Span One and Warder Hannetjie. It was because of the short-sightedness of Brille. That was the nickname he was given in prison and is the Afrikaans word for someone who wears glasses. Brille could never judge the approach of the prison gates and on several occasions he had munched on cabbages and dropped them almost at the feet of the warder and all previous warders had overlooked this. Not so Warder Hannetjie.

'Who dropped that cabbage?' he thundered.

Brille stepped out of line.

'I did', he said meekly.

'All right', said Hannetjie. 'The whole Span goes three meals off.'

'But I told you I did it', Brille protested.

The blood rushed to Warder Hannetjie's face.

'Look 'ere', he said. 'I don't take orders from a kaffir. I don't know what kind of kaffir you think you are. Why don't you say Baas. I'm your Baas. Why don't you say Baas, hey?'

Brille blinked his eyes rapidly but by contrast his voice was strangely calm.

'I'm twenty years older than you', he said. It was the first thing that came to mind but the comrades seemed to think it a huge joke. A titter swept up the line. The next thing

Warder Hannetjie whipped out a knobkerrie and gave Brille several blows about the head. What surprised his comrades was the speed with which Brille had removed his glasses or else they would have been smashed to pieces on the ground.

That evening in the cell Brille was very apologetic.

'I'm sorry, comrades', he said. 'I've put you into a hell of a mess.'

'Never mind, brother', they said. 'What happens to one of us, happens to all.'

'I'll try to make up for it, comrades', he said. 'I'll steal something so that you don't go hungry.'

Privately, Brille was very philosophical about his head wounds. It was the first time an act of violence had been perpetrated against him but he had long been a witness of extreme, almost unbelievable human brutality. He had twelve children and his mind travelled back that evening through the sixteen years of bedlam in which he had lived. It had all happened in a small drab little three-bedroomed house in a small drab little street in the Eastern Cape, and the children kept coming year after year because neither he nor Martha ever managed the contraceptives the right way, and a teacher's salary never allowed moving to a bigger house, and he was always taking exams to improve his salary only to have it all eaten up by hungry mouths. Everything was pretty horrible, especially the way the children fought. They'd get hold of each other's heads and give them a good bashing against the wall. Martha gave up somewhere along the line so they worked out a thing between them. The bashings, biting and blood were to operate in full swing until he came home. He was to be the bogey-man and when it worked he never failed to have a sense of godhead at the way in which his presence could change savages into fairly reasonable human beings.

Yet somehow it was this chaos and mismanagement at the centre of his life that drove him into politics. It was really an ordered beautiful world with just a few basic slogans to learn along with the rights of mankind. At one stage, before things became very bad, there were conferences to attend, all very far away from home.

'Let's face it', he thought ruefully. 'I'm only learning right now what it means to be a politician. All this while I've been running away from Martha and the kids.'

And the pain in his head brought a hard lump to his throat. That was what the children did to each other daily and Martha wasn't managing and if Warder Hannetjie had not interrupted him that morning he would have sent the following message: 'Be good comrades, my children. Co-operate, then life will run smoothly.'

The next day Warder Hannetjie caught this old man of twelve children stealing grapes from the farm shed. They were an enormous quantity of grapes in a ten gallon tin and for this misdeed the old man spent a week in the isolation cell. In fact, Span One as a whole was in constant trouble. Warder Hannetjie seemd to have eyes at the back of his head. He uncovered the trick about the cabbages, how they were split in two with the spade and immediately covered with earth and then unearthed again and eaten with split-second timing. He found out how tobacco smoke was beaten into the ground and he found out how conversations were whispered down the wind.

For about two weeks Span One lived in acute misery. The cabbages, tobacco and conversations had been the pivot of jail life to them. Then one evening they noticed that their good old comrade who wore the glasses was looking rather pleased with himself. He pulled out a four ounce packet of tobacco by way of explanation and the comrades fell upon it with great greed. Brille merely smiled. After all, he was the father of many children. But when the last shred had disappeared, it occurred to the comrades that they ought to be puzzled. Someone said: 'I say, brother. We're watched like hawks these days. Where did you get the tobacco?'

'Hannetjie gave it to me , said Brille.

There was a long silence. Into it dropped a quiet bombshell.

'I saw Hannetjie in the shed today', and the failing eyesight blinked rapidly. 'I caught him in the act of stealing five bags of fertilizer and he bribed me to keep my mouth shut.'

There was another long silence.

'Prison is an evil life', Brille continued, apparently discussing some irrelevant matter. 'It makes a man contemplate all kinds of evil deeds.'

He held out his hand and closed it.

'You know, comrades', he said. 'I've got Hannetjie. I'll betray him tomorrow.'

Everyone began talking at once.

'Forget it, brother. You'll get shot.'

Brille laughed.

'I won't', he said. 'That is what I mean about evil. I am a father of children and I saw today that Hannetjie is just a child and stupidly truthful. I'm going to punish him severely because we need a good warder.'

The following day, with Brille as witness, Hannetjie confessed to the theft of the fertilizer and was fined a large sum of money. From then on Span One did very much as they pleased while Warder Hannetjie stood by and said nothing. But it was Brille who carried this to extremes. One day, at the close of work Warder Hannetjie said: 'Brille, pick up my jacket and carry it back to the camp.'

'But nothing in the regulations says I'm your servant, Hannetjie', Brille replied coolly.

'I've told you not to call me Hannetjie. You must say Baas', but Warder Hannetjie's voice lacked conviction. In turn, Brille squinted up at him.

'I'll tell you something about this Baas business, Hannetjie', he said. 'One of these days we are going to run the country. You are going to clean my car. Now, I have a fifteen year old son and I'd die of shame if you had to tell him that I ever called you Baas.'

Warder Hannetjie went red in the face and picked up his coat.

On another occasion Brille was seen to be walking about the prison yard, openly smoking tobacco. On being taken before the prison commander he claimed to have received the tobacco from Warder Hannetjie. Throughout the tirade from his chief, Warder Hannetjie failed to defend himself but his nerve broke completely. He called Brille to one side.

'Brille', he said. 'This thing between you and me must end.

You may not know it but I have a wife and children and you're driving me to suicide.'

'Why don't you like your own medicine, Hannetjie?' Brille asked quietly.

'I can give you anything you want', Warder Hannetjie said in desperation.

'It's not only me but the whole of Span One', said Brille, cunningly. 'The whole of Span One wants something from you.'

Warder Hannetjie brightened with relief.

'I think I can manage if it's tobacco you want', he said.

Brille looked at him, for the first time struck with pity, and guilt.

He wondered if he had carried the whole business too far. The man was really a child.

'It's not tobacco we want, but you', he said. 'We want you on our side. We want a good warder because without a good warder we won't be able to manage the long stretch ahead.'

Warder Hannetjie interpreted this request in his own fashion and his interpretation of what was good and human often left the prisoners of Span One speechless with surprise. He had a way of slipping off his revolver and picking up a spade and digging alongside Span One. He had a way of producing unheard of luxuries like boiled eggs from his farm nearby and things like cigarettes, and Span One responded nobly and got the reputation of being the best work span in the camp. And it wasn't only take from their side. They were awfully good at stealing certain commodities like fertilizer which were needed on the farm of Warder Hannetjie.

The Coming of the Christ-Child

He was born on a small mission station in the Eastern Cape and he came from a long line of mission-educated men; great-grandfathers, grandfathers and even his own father, had all been priests. Except for a brief period of public activity, the quietude and obscurity of the life was to cling around him all his days. Later, in the turmoil and tumult of his life in Johannesburg, where Christmas Eve was a drunken riot, he liked to tell friends of the way in which his parents had welcomed the coming of the Christ-Child each Christmas Eve.

'We would sit in silence with bowed heads; just silent like that for a half an hour before midnight. I still like the way the old people did it . . .'

One part of the history of South Africa was also the history of Christianity because it was only the missions that represented a continuous effort to strengthen black people in their struggle to survive and provided them with a tenuous link between past and future. The psychological battering the older generations underwent was so terrible as to reduce them to a state beyond the non-human. It could also be said that all the people unconsciously chose Christianity to maintain their compactness, their wholeness and humanity for they were assaulted on all sides as primitives who were two thousand years behind the white man in civilisation. They were robbed of everything they possessed — their land and cattle — and when they lost everything, they brought to Christianity the same reverence they had once offered to tribe, custom and ancestral worship. The younger generations remembered the elders. Christianity created generations of holy people all over the land.

And so the foundations of a new order of life were laid by the missions and since the ministry was a tradition in his own family, its evolutionary pattern could be traced right from his great-grandfather's time when the lonely outpost mission church was also the first elementary school existing solely to

131

teach the Bible. From Bible schools, children began to scratch on slates and receive a more general education, until a number of high schools and one University College, attached to missions, spread like a network throughout the land. He was a product of this evolutionary stream and by the time he was born his family enjoyed considerable prestige. They were affluent and lived in a comfortable house, the property of the church, which was surrounded by a large garden. Their life belonged to the community; their home life was the stormy centre of all the tragedies that had fallen on the people, who, no matter which way they turned, were defaulters and criminals in their own land. Much is known about the fearful face of white supremacy; its greed and ruthless horrors. They fell upon the people like a leaden weight and they lay there, an agonising burden to endure.

One day there was — but then there were so many such days — a major catastrophe for the church. The police entered during the hour of worship (it was a point with all the white races of the land that no part of a black man's life was sacred and inviolable) and arrested most of the men as poll tax defaulters. The issue at that time was how people, with an income of twenty shillings a year could pay a poll tax of twenty shillings a year. There was only such misery in the rural areas, grandly demarcated as the 'native reserves'. Land was almost non-existent and people thrust back into the reserves struggled to graze stock on small patches of the earth. The stock were worthless, scabby and diseased and almost unsaleable. Starving men with stock losses were driven into working on the mines and the Boer farms for wages just sufficient to cover their poll tax. When their labour was no longer needed in the mines they were endorsed back to the mythical rural areas. There was no such thing as the rural areas left — only hard patterns of greed of which all the people were victims. It was impressed on people that they were guilty of one supposed crime after another and in this way they were conditioned to offer themselves as a huge reservoir of cheap labour.

Thus it was that the grubby day to day detail of human misery unfolded before the young man's eyes. Often only five shillings stood between a man and his conviction as a defaulter of some kind and it was his father's habit to dip deep into his own pocket or the coffers of the church to aid one of his members. That day of the mass arrest of men in church was to linger vividly in the young man's mind. His father walked up and down for some time, wringing his hands in distress, his composure shaken to the core. Then he had attempted to compose himself and continue the disrupted service, but a cynical male voice in the congregation shouted:

'Answer this question, Father. How is it that when the white man came here, he had only the Bible and we the land. Today, he has the land and we the Bible', and a second disruption ensued from weeping women whose husbands were among those arrested.

From habit the old man dropped to his knees and buried his face in his hands. The remainder of his congregation filed out slowly with solemn faces. He knelt like that for some time, unaware that his son stood quietly near observing him with silent, grave eyes. He was a silent, pleasant young man, who often smiled. He liked reading most and could more often than not be found with his head buried in a book. Maybe his father was praying. If so, his son's words cut so sharply into the silence that the old man jerked back his head in surprise.

'There is no God, father', the young man said in his quiet way. 'These things are done by men and it is men we should have dealings with. God is powerless to help us, should there even be such a thing.'

'Do you get these ideas from books, my son?' his father asked, uncertainly. 'I have not had the education you are having now because there was no University College in my days, so I have not travelled as far as you in loss of faith, even though I live in the trough of despair.'

This difference in views hardly disrupted the harmonious relationship between father and son. Later, people were to revere an indefinable quality in the young politician, not realising that the rose from the deep heart of the country, where in spite of all that was said, people were not the 'humiliated, down-trodden blacks' but men like his father. Later, he was to display a courage unequalled by any black man in the land. The romance and legends of the earlier history still quivered in the air of the rural area where he was born. Nine land wars had the tribes fought against the British. Great kings like Hintsa had conducted the wars, and in spite of the grubbiness and despair of the present, the older generations still liked to dwell on the details of his death. Hintsa had been a phenomenon, a ruler so brilliant that on his death his brains had been removed from his head so that some part of him could remain above ground to be revered and worshipped. It was a tradition of courage that his people treasured.

On graduating from university he did not choose the ministry as his career. Instead, he had one of those rare and elegant positions as Professor of Bantu Languages at the University of the Witwatersrand in Johannesburg. He was as elegant and cultured as his job and ahead of him stretched years and years of comfort and security. The black townships surrounding the city of Johannesburg absorbed genius of all kinds in astounding combinations. The poor and humble and the rich and talented lived side by side. Brilliant black men, with no outlet for their talents for management and organisation, were the managers and organisers of huge crime rings around the country with vast numbers of men in their employ. They flashed about the townships in flashy American cars of the latest design and sold their stolen goods at backdoor prices to the millions of poor, honest black labourers who served the city. Johannesburg was the pulsing heart of the land; everything of significance that happened in the country, first happened in Johannesburg. It was also the centre of the big labour shuttle; the gold mines stretching along the Witwatersrand with their exhaustible resources, needed thousands and thousands of black hands to haul those riches above ground. The city was complex, as international as the gold that flowed to all the banking houses of the world. It had also been the centre of ruthless exploitation and major political protest and it seemed to have aged in cynicism and weariness ahead of the rest of the country. It was a war-weary and apathetic world that he entered in 1948. It was as though people said: 'Ah, political protest? You name it, we've done it. What is it all for?' It took something new and fresh to stir the people out of their apathy and exhaustion.

Almost immediately he attracted a wide range of thinking men. Immediately, the details of his life attracted interest and he slipped into the general colour of the environment. But he carried almost the totality of the country with him. It wasn't so much his reading habits — there were hundreds of men there acquainted with Karl Marx and the Chinese revolution; there were hundreds of men there who wore their intellectual brilliance as casually as they wore their clothes. It was the fillers he provided on parts of the country that were now myths in the minds of urban dwellers — the strange and desperate struggles waged by people in the rural areas.

'I've just been reading this book on some of the land struggles in China after the revolution', he'd say. 'It was difficult for Mao Tse-Tung to get people to cultivate land because ancestor worship was practised there. I've seen people do the same thing in the Transkei where I was born. There was hardly any land left to cultivate but people would rather die of starvation than plough on the land where their ancestors were buried . . .'

Almost nightly there was an eager traffic of friends through his home. He enjoyed the circle of friends that gathered round him. He enjoyed knocking out his ideas against the ideas of other men and it was almost as though he were talking an unintelligible language. His friends no longer knew of the sacred values of the tribes — that all people had ever once wanted was a field where they might plough their crops and settled home near the bones of their ancestors. Like the young men of his circle, he was a member of the Youth League of an organisation that for forty seven years had been solely representative of the interests of black people. They had brought people out on the streets on protests and demonstrations. People had been shot dead and imprisoned. A strange hypnotic dialogue pervaded the country. It was always subtly implied that black people were violent; yet it had become illegal in the year 1883 for black men to possess arms. They had little beyond sticks and stones with which to defend themselves. Violence was never a term applied to white men, but they had arms. Before these arms the people were cannon fodder. Who was violent?

Year after year, at convention after convention this kindly body of the people's representatives mouthed noble sentiments:

'Gentlemen, we ought to remember that our struggle is a non-violent one. Nothing will be gained by violence. It will only harden the hearts of our oppressors against us . . .'

In 1957 there were more dead black bodies to count. Gopane village, eighteen miles outside the small town of Zeerust in the Transvaal was up until that year a quiet and insignificant African village. A way of life had built up over the years — the older people clung to the traditional ways of ploughing their fields and sent their children to Johannesburg, either to work or to acquire an education. In 1957 a law was passed compelling black women to carry a 'pass book'. Forty years ago the same law had been successfully resisted by the women who had offered themselves for imprisonment rather than carry the document. The 'pass book' had long been in existence for black men and was the source of excruciating suffering. If a man walked out of his home without his 'pass book' he simply disappeared from society for a stretch of six months or so. Most men knew the story. They supplied a Boer farmer for six months with free labour to harvest his potatoes. A 'boss-boy' stood over the 'prisoners with a whip. They dug out potatoes with such speed that the nails on their fingers were worn to the bone. The women were later to tell a similar tale but in that year, 1957, people still thought they could protest about laws imposed on them. Obscure Gopane village was the first area in the country where the 'pass book' was issued to women. The women quietly accepted them, walked home, piled them in a huge heap and burnt them. Very soon the village was surrounded by the South African Police. They shot the women dead. From then onwards 'pass books' were issued to all black women throughout the country without resistance.

Was it sheer terror at being faced with nameless horrors — who would shoot unarmed women dead? — or did the leaders of the people imagine they represented a respectable status quo? There they were at the very next convention, droning on again:

'Gentlemen', said speaker number one, an elderly, staid, complacent member of the community. 'Gentlemen, in spite of the tragedy of the past year, we must not forget that our struggle is essentially a non-violent one . . .'

He was going on like that — after all the incident had passed into history and let's attend to matters at hand — when there was a sudden interruption of the sort that had not disrupted those decorous boring proceedings for years. Someone had stood up out of turn. Speaker number one looked down his nose in disdain. It was the young Professor of Bantu languages. He was only in the Youth League section and of no significance.

'Gentlemen!' and to everyone's amazement the young man's voice quivered with rage. 'May I interrupt the speaker! I am heartily sick of the proceedings of this organisation. Our women were recently killed in a violent way and the speaker still requests of us that we follow a non-violent policy . . .'

'What are you suggesting that we do?' asked speaker number one, alarmed. 'Are you suggesting that we resort to violence against our oppressors?'

'I wish that the truth be told!' and the younger man banged his hand on the table in exasperation. 'Our fore-fathers lived on this land long before the white man came here and forced a policy of dispossession on us. We are hardly human to them! They only view us as objects of cheap labour! Why is the word *violence* such a terrible taboo from *our* side! Why can't we state in turn that *they* mean nothing to us and that it is our intention to get them off our backs! How long is this going to go on? It will go on and on until we say: "NO MORE!" ' And he flung his arms wide in a gesture of desperation. 'Gentlemen! I am sick of the equivocation and clever talk of this organisation. If anyone agrees with me, would they please follow me', and he turned forthwith and left the convention hall.

Everything had happened so abruptly that there was a moment's pause of startled surprise. Then half the assembly stood up and walked out after the young man and so began a new short era in the history of political struggle in South Africa. His political career lasted barely a year. George Padmore's book *Pan Africanism or Communism* was the rage in Johannesburg at that time and he and his splinter group allied themselves with its sentiments.

In spite of the tragedies of the country that year seemed to provide a humorous interlude to the leaders of the traditional people's movement. Their whole attention was distracted into ridiculing the efforts of their new rival; they failed to recognise a creative mind in their midst. The papers that were issued in a steady stream were the work of a creative artist and not that of a hardened self-seeking politician. The problems they outlined were always new and unexpected. They began slowly from the bottom, outlining basic problems.

'We can make little progress if our people regard themselves as inferior. For three hundred years the whites have inculcated a feeling of inferiority in us. They only address us as "boy" and "girl", yet we are men and women with children of our own and homes of our own. Our people would resent it if we called them "kwedini" or "mfana" or "moshemane", all of which mean "boy". Whey then do they accept indignity, insult and humiliation from the white foreigner . . .?'

A counter paper was immediately issued by the people's traditional movement:

'We have some upstarts in our midst who have promised to lead the people to a new dawn but they are only soft gentlemen who want to be "Sir-ed" and "Madam-ed". Who has led the people in mass demonstrations? Who is the true voice of the people . . .?'

They arranged for stones to be cast at him as he addressed public rallies and for general heckling and disruption of the proceedings. Yet during that single year he provided people with a wide range of political education such as the traditional people's movement had not been able to offer in all their long history. His papers touched on everything from foreign investment in the land which further secured the bonds of oppression, to some problems of the future which were phrased as questions:

Can we make a planned economy work within the framework of a political democracy? It has not done so in any of the countries that practise it today . . . We cannot guarantee minority rights because we are fighting precisely that group-exclusiveness which those who plead for minority rights would like to perpetuate. Surely we have guaranteed the highest if we have guaranteed individual liberties . . .?

The land could be peaceful for months, even years. There was a machinery at hand to crush the slightest protest. Men either fled its ravenous, insensitive brutal jaws, or, obsessed as a few men often are with making some final noble gesture or statement, they walked directly into the brutal jaws. It was always a fatal decision. No human nobility lit up the land. People were hungry for ideas, for a new direction, yet men of higher motivation were irresistibly drawn towards the machine. That machine was already gory with human blood and since it was only a machine it remained unmoved, unshaken, unbroken. Obsessed with clarifying a legality, he walked directly into the machine. The laws of the land were all illegal, he said. They were made exclusively by a white minority without consulting the black majority. It was a government of a white minority for a white minority; therefore the black majority was under no moral obligation to obey its laws. At his bidding thousands of black men throughout the land lay down their 'pass books' outside the gates of the police stations.

He had a curious trial. White security police had attended all his public meetings and taken notes but there were no witnesses for the State except one illiterate black policeman. He gave a short halting statement that made people in the public gallery roar with laughter.

'I attended a political gathering addressed by this man. I heard him say: The pass book. That is our water-pipe to parliament.'

There were sixty nine dead bodies outside a Sharpeville police station. He was sentenced to three years imprisonment for sedition. Then a special bill was passed to detain him in prison for life. He was released after nine years but served with so many banning orders that he could barely communicate with his fellow-men. Then he became ill ana died.

An equivalent blanket of silence fell upon the land. The crack-down on all political opposition was so severe that hundreds quailed and fled before the monstrous machine. It was the end of the long legend of non-violent protest. But a miracle people had not expected was that from 1957 onwards the white man was being systematically expelled from Africa, as a political force, as a governing power. Only the southern lands lay in bondage. Since people had been silenced on such a massive scale, the course and direction of events was no longer theirs. It had slipped from their grasp some time ago into the hands of the men who were training for revolution.

When all was said and done and revolutions had been fought and won perhaps only dreamers longed for a voice like that of the man who was as beautiful as the coming of the Christ-Child.

Dreamer and Storyteller

It was a winter morning. Just before dawn the stars shone like bright, polished blue jewels in the sky and a half-eclipsed moon suddenly arose with a hauntingly beautiful light. And it was a summer afternoon. The summer rain had filled my yard with wild flowers. I seemed to be living too, all the time, with animals' eyes — goats staring at me, cows staring at me, chickens staring at me. I slowly came alive with the background scenery. What have I said about the people of a free land, I who borrowed their clothes, their goats, their sunrises and sunsets for my books? Not anything very polite, it seems.

The wandering travellers of ancient times came unexpectedly upon people sitting around their outdoor fires.

'Who are you?' people asked.

'I am the dreamer and storyteller', they replied. 'I have seen life. I am drunk with the magical enchantment of human relationships. I laughed often. The big, wide free world is full of innocence . . .'

One imagines that those people always welcomed the storytellers. Each human society is a narrow world, trapped to death in paltry evils and jealousies, and for people to know that there are thoughts and generosities wider and freer than their own can only be an enrichment to their lives. But what happens to the dreamer and storyteller when he is born into a dead world of such extreme cruelties that no comment or statement of love can alter them? In the first place, in South Africa, who is one talking to? People there are not people but complexions and hair textures — whites, Coloureds, Indians and Africans. Who can write about that? Where is that wedge of innocence and laughter that resolves so many human ills?

It has surprised me, the extent to which creative writing is often regarded, unconsciously, as a nationalistic activity, and perhaps this expression of national feeling is rather the subdued communication a writer holds with his own society. I have so often been referred to as 'the Botswana writer', while in reality the Botswana personality isn't as violent as me. I wasn't born with the gentle inquiring eyes of a cow but amongst black people who always said, when anything went wrong: 'Why don't we all die?' And the subdued undertone was: 'since the white man hates us so much.'

Thought patterns change rapidly from one generation to another. We reformed the language of our parents because once the white man in South Africa started putting up notices 'For whites only', he also dispensed with normal human decencies — like 'please', and 'thank you' and 'I'm sorry' — while black people retained theirs as they have no benches to defend. It is impossible to translate a scene like this into human language. I once sat down on a bench at Cape Town railway station where the notice 'Whites Only' was obscured. A few moments later a white man approached and shouted: 'Get off!' It never occurred to him that he was achieving the opposite of his dreams of superiority and had become a living object of contempt, that human beings, when they are human, dare not conduct themselves in such ways.

It is preferable to have the kind of insecurity about life and death that is universal to man: *I am sure of so little*. It is despicable to have this same sense of insecurity — especially about a white skin — defended by power and guns. It seems to remove from them all fear of retribution for their deeds and it creates in the recipient of their wild, fierce, savage cruelty a deep sense of shock.

Day after day one hears of unbelievable slaughter in Ireland. A traveller from England passed my way. 'Why are people being killed like that in Ireland?' I asked. 'The Catholics are fighting for their rights', he said. 'They have always been discriminated against, never allowed to purchase their own homes and things like that. It's just like South Africa. There they call it racialism. In Ireland they call it religion.'

Every oppressed man has this suppressed violence, as though silently waiting the time to set right the wrongs that afflict him. I have never forgotten it, even though, for the purposes of my trade, I borrowed the clothes of a country like Botswana.

South Africa made white people rich and comfortable, but their ownership of the country is ugly and repellent. They talk about South Africa in tourist language all the time: 'This grand and sunny land', they say. The cheap, glaring, paltry trash of a people who are living it up for themselves alone dominates everything, infiltrates everywhere. If one is a part of it, through being born there, how does one communicate with the horrible? That is why South Africa has no great writer: no one can create harmony out of cheap discord.

It is impossible to guess how the revolution will come one day in South Africa. But in a world where all ordinary people are insisting on their rights, it is inevitable. It is to be hoped that great leaders will arise there who remember the suffering of racial hatred and out of it formulate a common language of human love for all people.

Possibly too, Southern Africa might one day become the home of the storyteller and dreamer, who did not hurt others but only introduced new dreams that filled the heart with wonder.

Acknowledgements

Of the twenty-one stories in *Tales of Tenderness and Power* three have apparently never been published before; they are 'Property', 'The General' and 'Son of the Soil'. The other nineteen have been published in literary journals, magazines and anthologies. They are: 'Let me tell a Story now . . .' in *New African*, Volume 1, no.9, 1962, Cape Town; 'Oranges and Lemons' in *London Magazine Stories 10*, edited by Alan Ross, London, 1976; 'Snowball' in *New African*, Volume 3, no.5, Cape Town, 1964; 'Sorrow Food' in *Transition*, Volume 30, no.6, 1967, Kampala; 'Village People, Botswana', 'The old Woman', 'Summer Sun' and 'The Green Tree' in *Classic*, Volume 2, no.3, Johannesburg, 1967; 'Tao' in *Freedomways*, Volume 7, no.1, 1967, New York; 'The Woman from America' in *New Statesman*, 26 August 1966, London; 'Chief Sekoto holds Court' in *Africa in Thunder and Wonder*: *Contemporary voices from African Literature*, edited by B. Nolan, New York 1972; 'A Power Struggle' in *Bananas*, 22 August 1980, 'A Period of Darkness' in *Kutlwano*, Volume 16, no.10, Gaborone, Botswana, October 1977; 'The Lovers' in *Wietie*, no.2. 1980, Johannesburg; 'The Prisoner who wore Glasses' in *London Magazine*, New Series, Volume 13, no.4, 1973, London; 'The Coming of the Christ-Child' in *Marang*, 1980– 1981, no.3; 'Dreamer and Storyteller', published as 'An African Story' in *Listener*, London, 30 November 1972. Head's original title 'Borrowed Clothes'. 'Chibuku Beer and Independence' in *New African*, Vol. 5, no. 9, 1966.